Interior Design Ideas

AURA
EDITIONS

Picture Credits

Acmetrack Ltd: 93(l); Brigitte Baert: 14, 107(r), 119; Paul Beattie: 24; John Bouchier: 102; Michael Boys: 97(r); Camden Studio: 56/7, 84/5; Candlelight Products: 7, 104; Gavin Cochrane: 85; Coloroll: 12(t&b), 15, 58, 90, 94/5, 114; Condor Public Relations: 72; Crescourt Loft Conversions: 69; Curtain Net Advisory Bureau: 1, 2, 4, 17, 49(l), 67, 103; Design Council: 93(r); Designers Guild: 6; Dorma: 8(r), 31, 40/1, 86/7, 88/9, 111; Dulux: 80/1; Ray Duns: 59, 105; Dux Interiors: 109; Faber Blinds (GB) Ltd: 51(l); Leo Ferrante: 32(l), 98(l); G Plan: 18/19, 26, 35, 41, 66, 81, 82, 108, 118/19; Dave King: 37(r), 49(l), 51(l&r), 53(t), 55, 73(b); Kingfisher Wallcovering: 79, 107(l); Di Lewis: 32(r); Max Logan Assoc: 53(b), 74, 91; Steve Lyne: 16(l&r), 65(l&r), 71; Nigel MacIntyre: 50(r); Frederick Mancini: 83, 94(t&b); Maples/Waring and Gillow: 13, 36, 76/7, 115; Bill McLaughlin: Back cover, 19, 25, 33, 42(l), 46(l), 70, 73, 75, 86, 90/1, 96, 98(cr&r), 112, 113(l&r), 116/17, 117; Michael Murray: 44/5; Nairn Vinyl Floors: 57(t); Martin Palmer: 46(r); Roger Phillips: Front cover, 78; Pilkington Flat Glass: 20(l); Polycell: 60; Malcolm Robertson: 23(l&r); Rotaflex Homelighting: 27(t), 30; Sanderson: 9(l), 10(r), 11, 21, 29, 37(l), 42(r), 45, 48, 52, 68, 88, 101; John Sharpe: 64(l&r); Solarbo Fitments: 20(r); Solid Fuel Advisory Service: 97(l); Jessica Strang: 38(l&r), 47, 50(l), 61(l), 63, 98(cl), 99(r), 110, 116

Author: Lindsey Stock
Editor: Alison Wormleighton
Designer: Caroline Dewing

Published by
Aura Editions
2 Derby Road,
Greenford, Middlesex

Produced by
Marshall Cavendish Books Limited
58 Old Compton Street,
London W1V 5PA

ISBN 0 86307 282 8

Typesetting and make-up by
Quadraset Limited, Midsomer Norton,
Bath, Avon

Printed and bound by
Grafiche Editoriali Padane S.p.A.,
Cremona, Italy

Contents

Introduction 5

CHAPTER 1
Alive with colour 6

CHAPTER 2
Better by design 13

CHAPTER 3
Lighting up time 21

CHAPTER 4
Cover story 31

CHAPTER 5
Frame-up 43

CHAPTER 6
First impressions 55

CHAPTER 7
All change 60

CHAPTER 8
Solid investments 74

CHAPTER 9
Finishing touches 96

CHAPTER 10
Living in style 106

Index 120

Introduction

Everyone wants their home to be an attractive, comfortable place that reflects their own personality and tastes. Sometimes, however, it's not so easy actually to achieve this. Many people haven't the least idea where to start in decorating and furnishing a home. Others have a good idea of the effect they are after but don't know how to go about achieving it. And there are still others, who know what they want *and* how to get it—but they'd like to learn more.

That is the joy of interior design. It is fun—in fact, quite compelling—regardless of whether you are a total beginner, perhaps doing up your first home, or an experienced and avid collector of ideas. What is more, the rewards are so great: a home you can be proud of, which is an expression of your own personality.

To put your own stamp of individuality on a place, you don't have to be starting from scratch, though that is a challenge in itself. There are innumerable ways to perk up a boring room, make a cold, uninviting place cozy, adapt an awkward room to suit your needs, add space without extending, or simply make a place more attractive and comfortable. What you need are ideas and enthusiasm, plus a little basic knowledge. That is the purpose of this book—to give you the guidelines and tips, advice and inspiration to create surroundings in which you feel completely at home.

A good place to begin is with colour (Chapter One). This can transform a room—or ruin it. It's colour first and foremost which gives a room its character—and which many people are nervous about using. The most fundamental part of interior design, however, whether you are starting from scratch or not, is the preliminary planning. You begin by analyzing the constraints you are working within, or, to look at it another way, the characteristics that make your home special. This is the subject of Chapter Two.

The next stage deals with the 'background' of a room: the atmosphere you create with lighting (Chapter Three) and the treatment of floors, walls and ceilings (Chapter Four). Windows and doors (Chapter Five) come into this category as well and provide a surprising amount of scope for adding interest and style to a home. But rooms should not be designed in isolation—the links between them are important. In many homes, these connections are provided by the hall, stairs and landing: the areas you are forever passing through, and which provide visitors with their first impressions of your home. Chapter Six deals with this often-neglected area, while Chapter Seven shows how to make the most of *any* room, from a rented bed-sit to a loft conversion.

Just as important as the decoration of a home are the furnishings and accessories. Chapters Eight and Nine show you how to choose and use these possessions to make your home really individual. Finally, to help you achieve that elusive quality 'style', Chapter Ten shows examples of rooms furnished in several different styles. By studying how these effects are achieved, you can learn to develop your own particular style—which is what interior design is all about.

CHAPTER 1

Alive with colour

Colour is what gives a room its character. It ties everything
together and makes a room come alive, while pattern adds
detail and interest.

room without colour has no identity. Even pale, neutral colour schemes using subtle tints have their own appeal.

What is colour?

Basically, colour is reflected light, which, when viewed through a prism, breaks up into the colour spectrum to form a rainbow effect. You might have noticed this when the sun is shining through the window and has somehow caught an unintentional prism, such as a piece of crystal.

All colours are made up of just three primary colours—red, yellow and blue. If you mix any two of these together in equal parts, you obtain the three secondary colours: orange (from red and yellow), green (from yellow and blue) and violet (from blue and red).

White is the result of all three primary colours being reflected, and black is the total absence of colour. Mixing white with a colour produces a 'tint', or pastel version of it, while mixing black with a colour produces a sooty, muted 'shade'. A 'tone' is either a tint or a shade, while a 'hue' is the pure colour, unadulterated by black or white. (Often, however, these terms are used very loosely, simply to mean 'colour'.)

Clear your mind of any prejudices you may have about colour before you begin to plan a scheme. The tone you may perhaps consider 'unlucky' green, or 'sickly' yellow, is just one example of an enormous number of other colours that come from the appropriate parent colour —some of which you may, to your surprise, find extremely pleasant.

The colour spectrum can be broken into two halves—warm colours and cool colours.

Warm colours are the reds, oranges and yellows. Cool ones are blues, greens and violets. Add proportions of white or black to any of these and you begin to see how infinite are the tones within one colour.

Thus each colour can be separated into millions of tones, and although paint manufacturers often offer massive selections of colours, they couldn't possibly compete with nature itself.

Different colours either harmonize with each other, because they lie near each other on the spectrum (such as orange and yellow), or contrast because they are placed far apart (such as red and green).

Colour moods

Colour can affect everyone to some degree, even to the extent of dictating our moods. Softer or stronger hues of the same colour can decrease or increase the effect.

Red is a fiery, dramatic colour associated with liveliness and alertness (used in industry, it signifies danger). It is also the warmest colour so can be used very successfully to give warmth to a room. Restaurants often use red in their colour schemes because it stimulates the appetite and the conversation! However, in large quantities, it can irritate, so should be used in association with a more calming colour such as green.

Orange is a reassuring, earthy colour, whether it is a rusty shade or one of the paler peach tones. At its brightest, it can be cheerful (like red), but also a little irritating in large quantities. Pale peaches and apricots are very good to live with and look extremely stylish combined with other pastel, calming colours.

Yellow is a cheerful, sunny and warm colour which needn't look garish if it's used to highlight certain areas. Dashes of yellow mixed with white make up a variety of creamy tones that are very useful for brightening up a dull room.

Left: When two primary colours—red and blue, red and yellow or blue and yellow—are mixed together, they produce a secondary colour: purple, orange or green. Above: A colour scheme using contrasting pastels gives a soft, romantic look to this room.

Right and below: Tones of green work particularly well together, and with a little yellow added they look both fresh and warm.

Green is cool, fresh and elegant. It represents nature most of all, bringing a little of the outdoors into the home. It can be used very successfully in most situations and, more than for any colour, variations of it look extremely good together. Dark, rich greens seem very sophisticated, while pale shades are refreshing and lighthearted.

Blue is a cool, fresh colour, often misrepresented as cold and sometimes badly used. It can make a bathroom look clean (especially since it conjures up the image of water), a living room spacious; and it can add dreaminess to a bedroom.

Violet is a powerful colour evocative of extreme emotions. This might be because of its make-up, a combination of opposites: dramatic red and cooling blue. It has, however, historical and regal associations and represents sensuality and wealth. It is probably best if used in pale tones or in small quantities.

White, in scientific terms, is all colours mixed together in equal proportions and therefore isn't really a colour at all! Home decorators, however, wouldn't be without it. It's an extremely efficient reflector of light and enhances other colours very well. Too much white, however, can look clinical and may need 'warming up' in some way. As white reflects maximum light, all colours put next to it will seem stronger, so take this into account when choosing colour schemes around it.

Black is the absence of all colour, but is as important a design medium as white. It can be a dramatic alternative that looks both stylish and sophisticated, or a good contrast to other colour areas.

Grey seems to be the newest and most original fashion colour to take hold in the last few years. It contrasts with most other colours extremely well, is very chic and adds masses of impact. Many think of it as a drab colour but, if used well, it can look terrific.

Pink must be mentioned for although it is a tint of red it is so unlike it in effect —compared to red, it is blissful, luxurious and very peaceful. It is often used in bedrooms to great effect, or to warm up a room lacking sunlight.

Brown is a very earthy colour and a natural contrast to paler, 'weaker' colours such as yellow. It doesn't have to look heavy if it's applied in small quantities or used with the right textures, such as cork or wood, which have a natural association with brown. It is quite a peaceful colour, and makes an excellent background for bright accent colours.

Choosing colours

The colour you choose may well depend on the choice available and the current trends, which tend to change every three years or so. However, ranges have extended and designs increased to such an extent that there is usually something for everyone. Budget does not necessarily play a part in choice, there being more really sophisticated designs at the cheaper end of the market than ever, and in colourways to suit everyone.

If you have a definite idea of what colour you prefer, so much the better. Don't be dictated to by others' choices—you'll be happier in the long run if you stick to your own preferences.

But if you want to be a little adventurous with colour and don't know where to begin, do not be put off by the myriad of paint, carpet, wallpaper and fabric samples you are likely to come across. Start by looking around you—in magazines, other people's homes, art galleries and, best of all, in nature.

Consider the feeling you're after. Light colours will give a fresh, spacious look, whereas dark colours make a room feel cozy. Rich colours like bottle green, dark rose, teal blue, lend elegance, while soft, restrained pastels add tranquillity, and bright colours liveliness.

You may find that you've picked a

Left and above: Don't be afraid to use a rich, strong colour like red in a decorating scheme. It can add a warm, sumptuous feeling and is especially effective in combination with white or a contrasting cool colour.

9

Above and right: Warm and peaceful, soft browns look lovely with apricot, sand, cream or white.

colour but are not sure about the particular tone you want to use. Make a collection of magazine cuttings, leaves, petals, crayons, paint samples—anything that will help—and study them for a while. After a time you will be able to whittle them down to three or four preferences and your awareness of colour will be improved at the same time. Do the same with your second or third colour choice, then you'll have different tones of two or three colours to mix, match or dispense with.

Aspect may be a determining factor when choosing a colour scheme. For example, a south-facing room which receives a lot of natural light and seems naturally warm, will look fine decorated in cooler colours. But a north-facing room, which never receives any direct sunlight and always seems cold, will be better decorated in warmer tones.

Colour schemes

Colours can of course be combined in an enormous number of different ways to produce a scheme that suits your taste and requirements, and there are no 'right' or 'wrong' ways of doing it. However, the one thing you should try to do is allow one colour to predominate, even slightly. Having equal quantities of two or more colours may produce an uneasy balance.

There are many ways you can achieve this. For instance, one of the simplest yet most effective types of scheme is to use one colour for the 'background' of a room (carpets, walls, curtains, even upholstery), then liven it up with bright accent colours for accessories like cushions and vases.

For a scheme that's very easy to live with, use a neutral colour like white, cream, beige or grey for the background, and pep it up with bright or strongly coloured accents.

Another alternative is the monochromatic colour scheme. This is based on one colour, with variations in shade and texture to keep it from looking dull. Done well, it can look very subtle and sophisticated.

If you prefer a bolder approach, you could bring in one or more other colours, not just for accents but also for a large area such as upholstery or curtains—so long as you use less of them than of the main colour. Additional colours could be contrasting (for example, terracotta with eau de nil, apricot with soft blue, yellow with lilac) or harmonizing (blue with green, for instance). Try, however, to keep the intensity and the lightness/darkness of the colours similar; otherwise the weaker one will just look washed out, and the stronger one overbearing.

Don't be afraid of using bright colours. It's not as difficult as it might seem to choose just the right amount of boldness that will bring the room alive.

Once you've whittled the choice down to a colour or two that you can say 'yes' to with absolute confidence, it is a good idea to make colour boards with samples of paint, wallpaper, fabrics and anything else that you intend to put in the scheme. Paint, wallpaper and fabric swatches are readily given if you ask, although you may have to pay a small sum for some fabric samples.

Even if you're still deciding between two colours, put samples of both of them on the board so you can see the overall effect and can cut one out later. Note how colours react to each other—red, for example, will look different placed next to blue than it will next to, say, cream. This goes for all colours.

Once your colour boards look satisfactory to you, start adding theoretical accessories to complete the scheme—such as pictures or lamps.

Don't think that everything must

Left: Different patterns can be combined very successfully when they have something in common, such as colours, to link them. Manufacturers have made it as easy as possible by designing co-ordinating patterns in the same colours.

colour match perfectly. A scheme that uses the same tone in everything will look fairly monotonous and be tedious to live with. But doubling or trebling the intensity of the colour in accessories, for instance, will add important touches of drama and interest. By the same token, don't be over-fussy about matching a particular shade exactly everywhere it appears in a room. Often a more in-teresting, less contrived effect is achieved when the match is not quite perfect.

If you have chosen a wallpaper with a multi-coloured pattern, you don't have to pick the predominant colour alone for carpet, paint or accessories. Using the less important colours along with the predominant one may make the room more interesting and give you greater scope to mix and match.

11

Pattern selection

If pattern picking fills you with dread, especially mixing different patterns, relax: all you need is confidence.

Experience helps, of course, but it isn't essential. The secret is to find a bond of some kind between designs. Colour is one of the best. As long as the colours (or the predominant colour) in two designs relate, anything is possible.

Some fabric and wallpaper manufacturers use the same tones of blues, reds, greens, and so on, throughout all their different designs, so the work is taken out of the client's hands. Some are linked by 'negatives'; for example, a design that has a white flower on a coloured ground may have a twin featuring a coloured flower on a white ground. Some patterned wallpaper and fabric ranges have two or three mini-print designs and one or two larger patterns which all relate.

If you want to be a little more adventurous, go for contrasts. Those that have the same depth of tone or the same proportions in pattern and colour will live quite happily with each other.

In fact, a simple rule of thumb which will practically guarantee success in pattern mixing is to make sure that the patterns have these two features: a clear link and a definite contrast.

Pattern can emphasize or visually decrease a room size. A large pattern makes a room look smaller, while a small one gives spaciousness. Pattern on a light background adds distance, whereas it draws walls inwards on a dark one.

Stripes are as effective in a room as they are to a figure! Thus, horizontals give height, verticals width.

Geometric designs can be linked together very well. Trellis designs are especially compatible because they have a strong linear bond—an example is where one large trellis design wallpaper is fixed below a dado rail and a smaller one above.

Above and right: Whereas floral patterns often look feminine and romantic, geometrics can create a modern, masculine effect. In both of these rooms, the colours provide the necessary link between the different patterns.

CHAPTER 2

Better by design

The size, shape and aspect of a room are the starting points in interior design. They form a set of challenges for you to work within, and make your home unique.

Right and far right: A fireplace is a natural focal point in a room, and furniture can be arranged to take maximum advantage of it.

*I*n an ideal world, we would all live where we chose, with orderly, spacious, beautifully designed rooms that fulfilled all our needs, without much effort or ingenuity on our part.

But this would mean homes without character, lacking in the little differences that make your own house or flat unique —problematic though you may think it is!

It's the time and effort spent planning and implementing a new scheme which makes a home your own. And that is also what makes interior design so satisfying. Thinking of your home as a 'shell', to be rearranged at will, is the first step to enjoying home design.

Many factors will dictate how you decorate: aspect, size, room proportion, budget, personal taste. All are important and all need to be considered and juggled together to come up with a happy solution.

If there are lots of people living under one roof, it is best to plan and arrange rooms so that there is a clearly defined route throughout the whole house. In other words, you need a logical way of getting from one place to another, without 'barriers'—furniture or otherwise— preventing easy access. If you're single and living alone, this won't matter so much, unless you're expecting a lot of social or family visitors.

The more doors there are in a room, the more 'traffic' routes you'll have to account for. Plan a furniture arrangement that either encourages the flow of human traffic, or directs it to advantage, allowing at least 60cm in width for each pathway.

Perfect planning
A good way to start is by thinking each room through individually, making lists of all items you consider a priority for each area—materials you want to decorate with, seating in the living room, beds in the bedrooms, table in the dining room, and so on. Some items you may already have, and accessories and luxuries can come later, leaving you with a certain number of items you'll have to buy.

By giving each priority a price limit and then adding them up, you can determine how much you may need to spend, and where you would least mind budgeting, if you've gone way over the top.

After doing this, you'll have a clearly defined view of what is most important and which areas can be left until later, when budget allows.

All this may seem time consuming, but it really will pay off in the final results.

The next step is to make scaled plans of each room you are decorating and/or changing, taking into account how certain rooms relate to their adjacent areas, for example the living room to the hall. Add any details like alcoves, doors, windows—anything, in fact, that restricts the way room furniture can be arranged.

Cut out templates (to scale) to represent furniture, lighting, rugs, etc. Measure everything carefully, estimating as accurately as possible those items you can't actually measure.

Once the plan is drawn and the shapes are cut out, the rest is fun. You can play around moving furniture and other items until you've found an arrangement that suits you and is a logical and efficient system.

Space needs
Some areas will need to be more spacious than others, depending entirely on personal needs. There is no reason why certain rooms should retain their given function—if swapping them would

improve space, light or traffic flow, then consider doing so. Dining rooms, living rooms and bedrooms can all be interchangeable, although kitchens and

bathrooms might have to remain as they are unless you have real cause for complaint and are ready for major internal work, plus plumbing changes.

*Above and right: When two rooms
have been knocked into one, the space
can be better utilized if one door is
blocked up, to remove a 'traffic lane'.
Far right: A window can be turned into
an attractive focal point in a room, even
if the view isn't particularly striking.*

Note where windows and doors are placed and consider whether these can be improved. A small window can be replaced with a larger one if needed, and a hinged door that opens into a room and thus restricts space can either be rehung to open outwards or replaced with a sliding door. This might be ideal for a particularly small bedroom where there's hardly space for a bed!

There may also be temporary internal walls, originally put in to increase the number of rooms, that can be removed to make two pokey rooms into one large one. A long, useless hall can be shortened to add space to a living room. Sometimes combined areas are better than separated ones, giving not only extra space but also more light, such as in a living/dining room.

Rooms where a partition wall has already been knocked down may still have two doors, one of which can be blocked up to remove a 'traffic lane'.

Scheming for space

The schemes you plan for your home may be dictated to by the type of house you live in.

Tiny modern houses tend to look box-like, especially if decorated in dark colours which violently change from room to room. Keep to fairly light, constant colours in each room, so there is an open, flowing atmosphere. There is no reason why you should not make subtle changes from room to room, but it might be wise to stick to some sort of constant bond throughout, whether it be carpet, wall colour or woodwork.

If rooms are large and airy already, you have much more choice and can plan each room to take on an individual character.

Colour alone can be used adeptly to stretch small spaces and shrink others (see page 42).

Furniture should be the right scale for each room, ensuring comfort all round—visually and dimensionally. An over-large sofa may seem like a wonderful luxury, but will become an irritation if it dominates the whole room.

Fabrics of curtains and furniture that blend well with their background will seem to look smaller, whereas those that contrast and stand out will look bigger.

Furniture arrangements are important —rows of chairs simply lined up against the wall may seem to save space, but will look awkward and without interest. It is better to create a focal point, or make the most of a natural one, such as a fireplace.

Once you have chosen the furniture for each room, make sure it will fit. This may sound more obvious than it is. An alcove may seem a perfect spot for a chest of drawers you've set your heart on and are sure will fit, but if you don't measure before you buy, you might find it misses by just a few centimetres. Measure *any* areas where furniture is to go.

Never make the mistake of assuming intended furniture will fit through your front door, either! Admittedly, removal and delivery men can do wonders with angles to get large pieces through small entrances, but they're not miracle workers if something will just not go through!

If your aim is to make rooms look as big as possible, then reduce the amount of furniture. Cluttered rooms not only look smaller, but can be positive hazards, especially if there are toddlers or elderly people around.

A tall piece of furniture or shelving unit that reaches almost up to the ceiling has a heightening effect. If you place an object of interest, such as a plant, on top of an already tall piece of furniture, it will lead the eye up, making the ceiling seem higher.

Windows can be made to look bigger

Right: The spaciousness of this large room has been emphasized by the use of a light, neutral colour scheme, wall-to-wall carpet and glass tables. By grouping the furniture into two separate areas, coziness is retained and access to the patio is not impeded.

by installing treatments higher or wider than the window itself (see page 44). Tall plants are also a heightening asset.

A long, narrow room may look a little like a corridor. You can offset this by adding a length of bookcases along the entire width of the smallest wall. In fact, running lengths of bookshelves along any small wall will make it look longer.

Big rooms can be made cozier by putting up wallpaper with large patterns. Televisions can be put into built-in units to save floor space, and stereo speakers can be fitted into corners at ceiling level.

Illusions of grandeur

You can enhance the illusion of size by simply using degrees of paint tones on different areas.

Anyone with a basic knowledge of art will know how the great masters use degrees of colour to create a sense of size, space, distance and light, and this can be applied to room schemes. If you use various shades of colour or pattern on different areas of a room you can give illusions of height, depth and width.

First consider the problems in proportion you are faced with. Is a room too tall? Is it too narrow? Too wide? By using different shades and by adding cornices, picture rails and dado rails, you can improve the effect considerably.

A tall, narrow room will look better if a picture rail is added and the area above the rail and across the ceiling is painted in a lighter shade than the area below.

Test this out for yourself—you don't have to be a great artist. Sketch out your room as if you were looking at it from one end, including all its proportional faults. Fill in the different areas—floor, walls, ceiling—with water colour paints or crayon and see how you can create an illusion. You may have to try out a few examples to find the best solution, but you should have fun doing it!

Open-plan living

Certain houses lend themselves naturally to open-plan living. Many cottages already have open-plan ground levels, usually giving these tiny homes a wonderfully spacious feel.

Complete open-plan living is a matter of choice, and whether or not there is a need for privacy within the home. Taking out all internal walls will certainly give a sense of space, although it seems a rather drastic step!

Certain structural changes will need to comply with building regulations, especially as some walls are important to the stability of the house, so you must always check first.

Mirror images

Mirrors can do a million things to increase size and give added light. A narrow hall can look twice the size if one wall is completely filled with a mirror, and it'll also make an ideal last-minute cosmetic check-point.

Mirrors are, in fact, an excellent way to reflect natural and artificial light. They can 'open up' dark areas and make a dull, narrow room look more interesting and spacious.

If you have small windows that don't let in much light, position mirrors so that they reflect the light source.

If you want to cover whole walls with mirror, sheets can be obtained from glass merchants. They will cut to any size and bevel and polish edges to order. Remember, however, that genuine mirror is very heavy and the wall must be able to take the weight.

Mirror tiles are easier to handle than sheets—and they aren't just for bathrooms. Fixing them up over a large area is a fairly laborious process, as they must be fitted in strict alignment to prevent distorted images. All vertical and horizontal joins must be parallel and the

surface on to which they are fixed completely flat. If it isn't, mount the tiles on to hardboard and mount this in turn on to battens fixed to the wall.

Be sure to position mirrors so as not to startle anyone. Mirror is very effective used on panelled doors, but, apart from the weight problem, sheet mirror is likely to break if the door is banged shut. A lightweight alternative is mirror sheeting consisting of tiny mirror tiles on a fabric backing. It is good for awkward or curved shapes as well, since it bends easily.

See-through solution

Clear glass is also useful in many ways within the home. Not only does it let light in through doors and windows, but

Below: A glass panel above a door allows a surprising amount of light through and is useful for brightening up dark areas.

Above left: Generous use of frosted glass makes this hall and porch feel light and airy without sacrificing privacy. Above right: Mirrored wardrobe doors are not only very handy when you're dressing, but also add an illusion of space to a bedroom or en-suite dressing room.

glass furniture will give a feeling of space and airiness in small rooms.

You can incorporate glass in many ways. Doors can have panels above, beside or integrated into them to admit extra light. Or, if you've a particularly dark room and can see no other solution, you can set an extra window in an internal wall. This will let light through from one room to another, and the window will form an attractive feature. You could even create a see-through display using dried flowers or small ornaments on slim glass shelves set into the frame sides.

Glass comes in a variety of colours and

finishes besides clear, and a trip to your local glass merchant is advisable before you make up your mind.

Stained or painted glass

Never replace original stained glass if it is in good repair. There's a revival of interest in this ancient art, and you can now find craftsmen who will repair or replace the odd broken pane—you may end up having the most envied windows in your street!

If you want to install stained glass, be prepared for it to be fairly expensive—it is, after all, very skilled work. Or consider having single stained glass

panes. Designs vary—from very beautiful, cathedral-style patterns to very simple, stylized ones that suit modern settings.

If you're feeling more ambitious, why not paint your own designs on to the windows? There are transparent glass paints especially for this (or you can use artist's oils or oil-based gloss, but these will not have the see-through effect of the special paints). There's no great skill in painting on glass—you simply use your fingers. If you tape the design on the opposite side of the pane of glass you can outline it from the inside, without needing particular artistic skills.

CHAPTER 3

Lighting up time

Never underestimate the importance of lighting in any room
scheme you are planning. It will affect the room more
dramatically than anything else you do.

Good lighting can enhance good points and hide bad ones. Yet we often take light for granted, or complain when there isn't enough, without doing anything about it except to change the bulb.

Well thought out lighting performs a combination of tasks. In areas like the bathroom, kitchen and utility room it should be purely functional, giving direct illumination without hazardous shadowy areas.

Other rooms, like living rooms, bedrooms and dining rooms, need a combination of lighting—cosmetic lighting to enhance the whole room scheme and act as a pleasant background, accent lighting to bring selected areas out of the dark and local lighting to illuminate specific working areas. There is no one right way to light every flat or house—each home has its own needs.

Advance planning

Combining such a selection of functions doesn't have to be as difficult and confusing as it sounds. If you are drawing up plans of the room/rooms showing intended furniture positions (see page 14), you should incorporate lighting needs before you even begin to hunt for fittings.

This may be based around existing power points, but you should ensure there are enough outlets for your requirements before you decorate—if not, work out how you can adjust what you have. For example, can you use an adaptor? Can you fix up a double spotlight to project light on to two areas at once?

Whatever adjustments you make, ensure that you never overload a circuit. If you do need some rewiring, or think you might, you should contact a qualified electrician, who will be able to advise you as to exactly what is necessary and will also estimate the cost.

Lighting fixtures

Make yourself familiar with the various lighting terms and the types of fixtures available, before you buy. Here is a comprehensive guide to help you.

General lights are those that give unrestricted light from a source such as a tungsten (incandescent) bulb or fluorescent tube. They include pendant or ceiling lights, paper or glass globes, standard or table lamps and strip lighting.

The type of shade used and the wattage of the bulb will determine how much light is actually thrown out, but relying on an existing central fitting to light one room adequately is a mistake. The effect will be flat and monotonous, and insufficient for areas where concentrated light is needed, such as for reading.

Table lamps provide concentrated areas of general light, usually pleasant in effect, according to the choice of shade. Lamp bases come in a wide variety of styles to suit everyone. Lamp shades generally spread more light if they have a pale coloured interior or lining. Make sure the shade is in proportion to the base —too small and the lamp will look silly, too big and it will appear top-heavy.

Jointed reading lamps using a general source of light are adequate for reading purposes if the beam is aimed directly at the working area by a shaped hood.

Wall fittings are another source of general light and there are a number of designs available to fit in with specific period styles. New wall light points must be fitted before any decorating takes place, as the wiring must be channelled into the plaster.

Directional lighting includes all forms of lighting where the beam is directed on to a particular spot by means of a hood, baffle or reflector shield; picture lights are one example. This covers areas of general lighting such as certain pendant and standard lamps and spotlights.

Spotlights give out a strong beam of controlled light wherever directed and can be either fixed or adjustable. They come in singles or groups of two, three or more, fixed on to a track. Conventional models take an ordinary tungsten bulb but more sophisticated designs take special bulbs with integral reflectors to intensify the beam. Some spotlights have clip-on or magnetic plates so they can be fixed on to a table top and pointed in any chosen direction.

Spotlights are ideal for kitchens where beams of light can be used for specific working areas, but should not be relied on as the only source of light. Spotlights can also be used as an alternative to a central light pendant fitting since they can be wired up through the same ceiling rose.

Downlighters and uplighters, as their names suggest, are lights that throw beams of light down to the floor or up to the ceiling.

Usually in the form of metal canisters of various shapes, they can be recessed or semi-recessed into a surface, such as the ceiling, or mounted on top.

They are usually fitted with an anti-glare device—in the case of downlighters this ensures comfort for anyone standing directly beneath the beam of light.

Some downlighters are specially designed for lighting a specific object or area, such as those for paintings. Some uplighters are good for 'wallwashing'—literally washing the wall with a wide beam of light. The effect of this is quite simply a matter of taste, but might be the solution if you're looking for a dramatic effect. Wallwashing will not affect other lighting in the same room.

Uplighters and downlighters are often used to illuminate a particular plant or treasured piece of furniture—but do make sure that the heat from the lamp will not damage a surface.

Below: Fluorescent tubes provide good illumination over a large area and are economical to run. However, their light is fairly cold and harsh unless you choose the warm white variety.

Left and above: Downlighters give a good general light, and the fittings themselves are attractive. They are easily set into a false ceiling like this slatted timber one suspended from the joists.

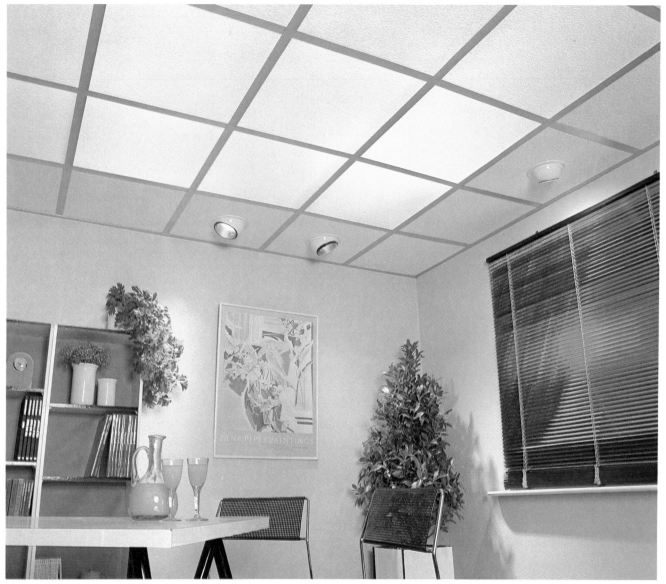

Above: An illuminated false ceiling using fluorescent tubes and downlighters gives a bright new look to a room.

voltage lamps need special dimmers that must be installed by a qualified electrician.

There are three types of dimmer—rotary action models with control knobs; touch-control dimmers; and remote control dimmers (which use an infra red hand control box). Plug-in models are also available.

Lighting schemes

The most effective and impressive lighting uses both shade and light in balanced proportions. A room that looks dull with all-over, even lighting can look beautiful and inviting with a finely balanced mixture, capitalizing on all the effort that has gone into decorating the room.

Areas of shade do not have to be pitch dark—gentle shadows combined with soft lighting create atmosphere and coziness. Dramatic schemes might benefit more from a combination of bright spots of light with quite imposing shadows. Functional lighting fixtures can be switched on as necessary.

Light room schemes reflect light, while dark ones absorb it. So in a room decorated with creamy pastels or white, for example, less intense light is needed than, say, in a richly patterned room using navy blue and burgundy.

The amount of natural light that enters a room also makes a difference—you'll know after a period of time which rooms receive most light and at what times of day. This will determine not only the type of décor you choose, but the amount of artificial lighting you need—obviously a south-facing bedroom that has two large windows and lots of light all day will need less supplementary light at certain times of the day than a north-facing living room with one window.

Choose bulbs with some care—you can create quite a different glow with

Dimmer switches are considered by many interior designers to be vital components in a lighting scheme. They allow great flexibility, allowing you to change the mood of the lighting at any time. And they control spotlights and other forms of directional lighting as effectively as they will adapt central or lamp lighting.

If you want to use a dimmer to control several lights, check it has the correct wattage rating—one dimmer will usually control up to four 60 watt bulbs or two 100 watt. Fluorescent lights and low-

different bulbs—and they come in various hues. Whereas a clear bulb will emit a fairly harsh, unrestricted light, a pearl-effect will be much softer and warmer. Try a few out—if some aren't right, they'll still be useful in other places.

Strategically placed lamps will give soft accent lighting but the choice of shade is important. If possible, ask if you can see what a lamp is like switched on. This will be easier in specialist lighting shops where displays are usually lit anyway, but try to remove one light from a whole display so that you can see its proportion and effect properly. This applies to all light fittings.

Check whether the light takes a bayonet or screw fitting bulb and what size is needed. Bayonet fitting bulbs come in a variety of colours, but screw fittings do not. Take this into account if you're thinking about swapping colours every so often.

Standard lamps have come back into fashion in recent years and styles have improved considerably. You can still buy models with 'drum' type shades—rather like elongated table lamps—but there are also lots of more modern designs that use directional lighting and are ideal for those who want to read from the comfort of an armchair. Some are quite stunning but unfortunately tend to be rather costly. If you've set your heart on a lamp like this, why not wait until you have enough money instead of making do with something you might consider second-best?

Ceiling fittings don't have to be restricting. There are pendant style shades to suit everyone, from metal coolie designs in various sizes and colours to tasselled broderie Anglaise neo-Victorian shapes. But if you want to dispense with a pendant shade, you can fit a track of spotlights using an existing ceiling rose.

Lighting can visually change the proportions of a room in various ways. Beams of light directed at a ceiling, for example, will make it look higher, whereas downlighters or spots fixed at low level will make a high ceiling seem lower.

Suppress any urges to buy novelty lamps or lights on a whim, and avoid impulse purchases of decorative lamps which you haven't planned into your lighting scheme. The light may simply take up valuable space, do little to enhance the room's lighting and be a regretted drain on your finances.

Many areas benefit from the addition of concealed lighting, for either practical purposes, decorative accent or a combination of the two. Wall cabinets and wardrobes often come with their own lighting; or you can add it yourself fairly easily.

Make the most of traditional-style curtains by hiding a light source behind a pelmet—but first make sure that the fittings are suitable and that heat from

Below: This old-fashioned oil lamp has been converted to use electric power to provide a decorative light source. Reproduction 'oil lamps' are also available which are already discreetly electrified.

bulbs will not damage nearby materials.

Alcoves can be fitted with fluorescent tubes or tungsten fixings, concealed behind false wall panels—what better way to find books and records easily or display plants and treasured collections at their best?

Some manufacturers make lampshades to match wallpaper and fabric collections. Unfortunately, these tend to be in a limited choice of shapes. The alternative is to cover your own. A variety of furnishing fabrics, and even dressmaking fabrics, are suitable, but those with a certain amount of 'give' are best as they are the easiest to work with and are less likely to wrinkle once they're fixed on to the shade frame.

Front halls can be lit to match in with other rooms' moods—downlighters are ideal—but make sure there is subsidiary lighting by the telephone, near coat hooks, by mirrors and above the front door.

Dining room lighting

The type of lighting required for dining depends on what sort of meal you are preparing. For children's meals you will need a brighter, more practical light than for dinner parties, where a soft, romantic glow is perfect.

Rise and fall pendant lights over the table are ideal as they will allow for flexibility—intimate lighting when pulled down, good general lighting (out of the reach of tiny hands) when pushed up to their full height and somewhere in the middle if the table is used for other jobs like writing or sewing. Rise and fall fittings must be positioned to illuminate the food without glaring into the eyes of the diners.

A comfortable bulb wattage is important. Dull light means the diners can't see what they're eating, while bright light means a lack of atmosphere

—so aim somewhere in the middle. A dimmer switch is a good way to control this.

Rise and fall triple spotlights can take the place of pendant shades, but they too must be positioned for comfort.

If a ceiling fitting is in an awkward place, extend the flex and suspend it from a ceiling hook directly over the table. If you change the position of the dining table, you can also move the ceiling hook —though if you do it often, you'll have a collection of tiny holes in the ceiling to fill up.

Round tables need only one light, but a

Far left: A combination of different types of lighting, including uplighters, spotlights and standard lamps, provides dramatic mood lighting and defines the different areas of a room. Left above: In this fairly large room, a track of spotlights has been run in an L-shape so that fixtures around the room receive equal attention. Light has been carefully directed to highlight pictures and books. Left below: Spotlights come in a number of styles. You can even get three mounted on a single base.

Above: For reading in bed, directional lighting is better than table lamps. Here a pendant fitting can be swivelled into position, and switched on or off without getting out of bed.

long, rectangular table may need two for comfortable dining.

Practicalities

Lighting is a very economical source of power. Don't skimp because you think it will save on electricity bills.

Lighting accounts for only 7 per cent of an average household's electricity bill; in one hour, an electric drill or a vacuum cleaner will use the same power as four 100-watt bulbs. A television will use the same as eight 100-watt bulbs.

Safety is of paramount importance with anything to do with electricity. Never overload a circuit and always ensure there is sufficient ventilation for recessed or enclosed fittings, to avoid a dangerous build up of heat.

Potential accident areas should be well-lit, and landings and staircases should have two-way switches between floors.

Cellars should have maximum lighting, with a switch at the top of the stairs for instant illumination. A two-way dimmer switch is ideal if the cellar has been converted into any room other than a store.

Never watch television with all the lights off, as this can cause eye strain.

Every room should have at least one light that is turned on by a switch by the door. This doesn't have to be the central light—the circuit could be wired up so that one or more of the other lights in the room can be switched on.

Simply using a long flex on a lamp positioned out of reach of a socket is not a solution to problems—especially if it creates a hazardous potential trip wire. It would be better to add new sockets around the room where necessary.

Check that fittings carry a safety label —it's inadvisable to buy any that don't. Make sure you know before leaving the shop how to change the bulb and clean the fitting properly; dirty bulbs and shades absorb light and don't work efficiently. Most shades carry a label indicating the safest maximum bulb wattage—never exceed this.

Sight for sore eyes

Table lamps are inefficient as bedside reading lamps—special angled reading lights or directional fittings such as spotlights are much better.

Two wall-mounted spots over a double bed mean that each partner can turn his or her light on and off without having to disturb the other.

Ideally, right-handed people should read by light thrown over the left shoulder, and vice versa for left-handed people. Reading light should be a reasonable distance from the page, or it will be too bright.

For television viewing, make sure that lights are not placed on top of televisions, which disturbs the contrast, or directly by those who are viewing, to avoid reflections on the screen. The ideal spot for a light is to one side and a little apart from the set.

Seen in a proper light

Lighting can be a little too honest sometimes, but if you're putting on make up, shaving, styling hair and so on, the better you can see yourself, the more satisfying the results!

It isn't a good idea to have lighting above a mirror as it will cast shadows on to the face. Strips of lighting down both sides are ideal, or if you want to go for something a little more spectacular, theatre-style make-up bulbs around the mirror couldn't be more revealing! Fluorescent lighting is best avoided in bedrooms; tungsten fittings are far more comfortable.

Children's lighting

The type of light needed in a child's bedroom depends on the child's age.

Teenagers need a combination of lighting: good general light combined with working lamps for studying or reading, plus light in which they can relax, play records or chat to friends. Every teenager likes to be treated like an adult, so spotlights or downlighters will be most appreciated. These can be fitted with coloured bulbs to add the occasional touch of modern glamour.

Younger children's light fittings, especially toddlers', should be child-proof as far as possible. Special safety plugs will

Left: A pretty reproduction brass lamp with frilled glass shade adds atmosphere and intimacy to this bedroom.

29

keep out inquisitive little fingers, but the fewer plug-in appliances there are, the better.

In a bedroom which also serves as a playroom, the floor should be well lit. Dimmer switches are safer than normal switches and can be turned up for games, and down to provide that added night security that some children need. Also available are some delightful specially designed night lamps in all kinds of fun shapes.

Good alternatives
Oil lamps remain a fashionable lighting alternative for special occasions, although the illumination produced isn't sufficient for functional purposes.

A traditional or reproduction oil lamp provides a soft, moody light that is ideal for dinner parties. Their advantage lies in the fact that the brightness can be altered (and they're also very useful during power cuts).

Candles are dearly and rightly loved—romantic candlelit dinners will always be popular. Make sure that they are placed in proper holders; these are not only safer but also less messy than improvised alternatives like old saucers. Never encourage children to play with candles or allow them to have them in their room except during power cuts, and then they should ideally be encased in safety enclosures, like lantern-style holders.

Light years ahead
Developments in the lighting industry are always on the move. Newest in this field are special filaments that last about six times longer than the average tungsten bulb. Although available to the consumer now, they are still in the process of being developed and there are many improvements to be made.

They come in different sizes, so will fit most lamps, and although they're not beautiful to look at, they're extremely tough. At present, however, they are heavy and extremely expensive compared to standard bulbs.

One type has been specially made as a cool burner so that it can be used very close to fabric lampshades without the danger of burning.

Right: Spotlights provide good lighting in children's bedrooms and are well out of the way of inquisitive fingers. In this room the track is positioned towards the centre of the room, and the spotlights directed where they can be of optimum use—into the cupboard and over the cot.

CHAPTER 4

Cover story

Floors, walls and ceilings are integral parts of a decoration scheme. As the largest and most visible parts of a room, they form an important background for the furnishings.

Above: Wood strip flooring looks warm and elegant in any room. Right: Wooden flooring in a herringbone pattern is a good way of adding interest and texture.

ow a scheme will eventually look is determined to a large extent by budget, as well as by existing furniture, and the style and size of the house.

Although walls are extremely important, the floors should be your first priority. More money may have to be spent to create the right effect (and a mistake may be an extremely costly exercise).

Floor coverings

Carpet and vinyl may be the most obvious ways to cover a floor, but there are many alternatives. Among these are cork, stone, quarry tiles, ceramic tiles, sisal and rush matting, wood, rubber and many more.

However, before you even begin to shop around for flooring, study the condition of the existing floor.

Wood floors

If you live in a newly built, modern house you will have little choice but to cover the floors. If, however, you live in an older house or flat, you may have wooden or parquet floors that can be left bare and beautiful, with a little care.

Not all wood floors are suitable—some may be in such a bad condition that they're not worth the hard work it would take to restore them. The key to success is that the floor itself should be in excellent condition. If you have draughty gaps, dust traps, heat loss or rotted boards, it would be wise to think again. But if these problems do not exist or are so minor that the restoration work will seem worth it, then sanded, sealed and polished bare boards will be the envy of all your friends.

Natural boards can be finished in various ways. Wood stains come in a variety of colours and create marvellous effects. If you want to take it one step

further, try stencilling patterns on to the boards. Quite simple designs are available from craft shops, or you can buy sheets of stencilling paper from which you cut your own designs. Stencils can be used in conjunction with rugs—use the stencilling as a border around the rug, or around the skirting board.

If all this natural, traditional beauty appeals but your floor is plain old concrete, you could consider having a new wooden floor laid. Parquet is the most common type, but there is also strip flooring and even herringbone; all come in a choice of different woods. As a wood floor is a major investment, it is worth having it installed by a skilled flooring contractor—though there is a type of strip flooring that comes in large pre-

assembled panels and can be laid by someone reasonably competent at diy.

Vinyl flooring

Vinyl is the all-round, hard-wearing floor covering. It need not be restricted to kitchens and bathrooms, although it undoubtedly has very durable qualities ideally suited to those areas.

Successful use can be made of vinyl in areas like hallways and passages and other places that receive rough treatment. In fact, designs have become so sophisticated that there is no reason why vinyl cannot be used in bedrooms, children's room or anywhere else. Added comfort can be provided by a selection of non-slip rugs.

Vinyl is quite easy to lay, but the floor

Left: Ceramic floor tiles add elegance and blend well with period furnishings. Though cold to the touch and rather hard on the feet, they are so good-looking that people are usually willing to overlook those drawbacks.

surface must be perfectly flat to ensure a good finish. If it isn't, then you'll have to lay a covering of hardboard underneath the vinyl.

Carpets

Good quality carpet may seem expensive once you've worked out the wall-to-wall costs, but it is a worthwhile investment. It will last longer, feel warmer and seem more luxurious than cheaper varieties.

However, *all* carpet should be laid properly and it's advisable to employ a qualified carpet fitter, unless you're confident about your own abilities.

All carpet should be fitted over a suitable underlay—there really is no point in spending lots of money on the carpet and skimping elsewhere. A good underlay will ensure even wear and will in fact improve the performance of the carpet. Professional fitters also put a layer of felt paper underneath the underlay to increase noise reduction and prevent heat loss.

Before you pinpoint the exact carpet you're going to buy, you must assess the

Right: Carpet comes in a range of colours, widths, weights, piles, fibres and methods of construction, so there is bound to be one that is right for you, whatever your needs.

wear and tear it is likely to receive. For example, the stairs, hall and living room floors will get rougher treatment than, say, bedrooms. So a deep, soft pile carpet, though ideal in the bedroom, is not suitable in other areas.

Most manufacturers make carpets in different qualities, usually in the same colour range, so you can order for a variety of areas without necessarily changing the colour, should you decide to have wall-to-wall uniformity throughout the house.

Designs, patterns and colours vary tremendously and there are a few tips it might be wise to follow. Strong patterns are best used only in large rooms, but beware of choosing a pattern that you are likely to ·become tired of before its life span is finished.

Plain colours are adaptable and do not restrict you when you want to change the scheme later on. Plain coloured carpet will make small rooms look more expansive, and if you want to add pattern you can use a selection of rugs.

Carpet tiles, though never as luxurious as fitted carpet, are perfect if there's a tight budget to be considered. They're hardwearing and come in a variety of patterns and colours. If one particular area of tiles becomes worn, it's easy to replace the worn tile, but it is best to switch the tiles around from time to time to prevent concentrated wear.

To help you judge whether a particular carpet is suitable for your needs, here is a guide to their main characteristics.

The weight or density of a carpet affects how well it will stand up to regular use, and is indicated by the CP (Carpet Performance) rating on the label. This is either A (Extra Heavy Wear), B (Very Heavy Wear), C (Heavy Wear), D (General Wear), E (Medium Wear) or F (Light Wear). You may still come across carpets classified in the old way:

from 1 to 5 (Light Domestic, Medium Domestic, General Domestic, Heavy Domestic and Heavy Contract).

The construction of a carpet also determines its wearability. Carpets are either woven, tufted or bonded. *Woven* is the most expensive, as the backing is woven at the same time as the pile, producing a very dense, hard-wearing carpet. There are two types of woven carpets: Axminster, which is used for multi-coloured carpets, and Wilton, which is used for plain carpets and patterned carpets with no more than five colours. In *tufted* carpets the tufts are inserted into the backing and held in place with adhesive. Less expensive than weaving, this method is used for the vast majority of British carpets. The third method of construction is *bonding*, in which the pile is bonded (often by heat-fusing) on to a backing. Bonded carpets are usually quite inexpensive.

The texture of a carpet is determined by its pile, which is either *loop pile* (consisting of a series of uncut loops, such as in cord carpets), *cut pile* (in which the loops are cut), or *cut-and-loop pile* (a combination of the two, producing an interesting textured effect). Well-known types of cut-pile carpets are *shag pile*, which is made from very long strands (but is inclined to tangle and mat and is only suitable for light use); *velvet pile*, which has a very short, smooth, even-cut pile (and tends to show shading or 'pile pressure' rather quickly); and *twist pile*, in which the yarn is twisted for a hard, springy effect.

The fibre a carpet is made from is also important. *Wool* is the finest (and most expensive), as it is very resilient, resists dirt and looks good for a long time. Undyed wool is the traditional fibre for those natural-looking, neutral-coloured Berber carpets. Synthetic fibres, however, have been greatly improved in recent years. *Nylon* is extremely hard-wearing, and is less prone to static electricity than it used to be, but it can soil badly. Carpets made from 80% wool/20% nylon combine the best of both worlds, and are very commonly used for areas that get a lot of wear, such as stairs and living rooms. *Acrylic* looks more like wool than any other man-made fibre, is just as hard-wearing but tends to flatten with heavy foot traffic; it soils more easily than wool, but is easily cleaned. *Polypropylene* is another hard-wearing fibre. Resistant to stains and easy to clean, it is suitable for medium wear, and is often used for cord carpets and bathroom carpets. *Polyester* on its own is only suitable for light-wear uses but is often blended with other fibres.

All kinds of rugs

Rugs can be exotic additions to any room. They are especially versatile because they can be moved around at will and taken away should you decide to move home.

Rugs will introduce colour and pattern to a scheme and some are even large enough to cover an entire floor. There are many types of rugs available, ranging in price from very inexpensive to extremely dear. Three of the more commonly available are Persian, Berber and Dhurrie rugs.

Persian rugs use ancient patterns and are hand knotted from silk and wool on a woven base. They tend to be very expensive.

Berber rugs are traditionally made in the Sahara from natural, undyed wools in

Below: Rugs can be used in an enormous number of ways, on bare floors or on top of carpet. They are a good way to define different areas of a room, and are particularly well suited to old-fashioned rooms like this one.

Above: Exposed brickwork looks good in modern-style rooms and can be either painted, or left natural and coated with clear masonry sealer.

cream, brown or grey stripes. They range considerably in price.

Dhurrie rugs are woven in India in bright, pretty colours, and are relatively inexpensive. They're very good for throwing over a sofa or chair as well as covering floors.

Sisal, cord and rush matting

These provide good alternatives to carpet, if a little scratchy! They are warm, cheap and can be cut easily to fit awkward shapes.

Wall coverings

What you put on your walls may make or break a room scheme. There are many ways in which you can cover them,

although paint and paper are the most obvious, easy and economical choices.

The condition of the wall may determine how you go about decorating—extremely uneven walls will not take paper unless you first apply lining paper, or in extreme cases a layer of hardboard.

Paper or painted borders are great for adding a little charm to a room. Many wallpaper books have matching borders that co-ordinate with paper designs, or you can simply buy the border for use on a painted wall. Some of the most charming designs are those especially for children. Or you could stencil your own if you prefer.

Exposed brickwork

You might want to try exposing your brickwork—either in parts or on a whole wall. Bare brickwork can be texturally interesting and create a feature in a room, for example on the chimney breast.

Varnish added to bare brick brings out its natural colour and prevents the brick from crumbling or getting dusty. Emulsion paint is also good for brickwork and there are a variety of special brick paints in strong colours to enhance texture and colour.

Stripping plaster to expose brickwork is a messy, tiring and long job—and a disaster if you don't like the results, or there are no bricks underneath anyway! To be sure, remove a wall-mounted electrical socket (don't forget to turn the mains switch off first!) or prise away a section of a skirting board. Examining the brick in this way will also indicate whether it's worth exposing.

If, however, you can't see any brick but are convinced it's there, you'll have to drill into the wall and examine the dust, or strip a small experimental area of plaster.

If bricks were originally intended for plastering, they'll probably not be very

handsome—this is especially the case in modern houses.

Stone or brick cladding kits may be the alternative—although never as good as the real thing.

Paint options

Far from being a limiting choice of wall decoration, paints are available in such a wide range of colours that you will actually be spoiled for choice. And application couldn't be simpler.

With some paints you can obtain small 'sample' pots at little cost to take home and try out on a small area before you decide.

Developments in the paint market have improved quality and performance of paints. Today's paints can be divided into six main types.

Primers are surface sealers which help finishing coats to adhere properly. They are used on new and exposed wood and metal. As well as general-purpose/universal primer, there are a number of specialist primers for different surfaces.

Undercoats form the middle layer between primer and topcoat. They are normally used when building up a paint system on bare wood, and also when re-coating a previously painted surface in a lighter colour, although they are not necessary beneath a non-drip gloss paint.

Emulsions are water-based paints, still popular for walls and ceilings. They are relatively cheap, quick-drying and available in a variety of finishes such as silk, satin or matt.

Eggshells are oil-based paints that give a very durable, easily cleaned, almost matt finish. Unfortunately, colour ranges tend to be limited.

Gloss is the most commonly chosen oil-based paint for woodwork and metal, giving a shiny, easily cleaned finish. Full (high) gloss and non-drip (low) gloss versions are available.

Special effects

Once you have decided on a colour scheme and which type of paint each area requires, think about any 'special' effects you want to create. If you live in an older, period-style house, remaining picture rails, dado rails, cornices and panels can be picked out in toning colours or emphasized in various ways to give the room interest.

If you don't have original features such as these, you can buy reproduction plaster mouldings (although if you live in a very modern house, such additions may not look in keeping with the character of the house).

Trompe l'oeil (a hand-painted mural) is an original way to brighten up or add

Left: Full use has been made of the dado in this small dining room, to create a beautifully co-ordinated decorating scheme which is echoed in the soft furnishings. Above: Reproduction plaster mouldings can be used to add interest and character in a traditional-style home.

Above and right: Hand-painted trompe l'oeil murals are great fun, and are a perfect way to brighten up a child's bedroom.

humour to a room, and add an ingredient of individuality. Well-chosen designs can help to hide uneven surfaces and odd-shaped ceilings.

You can paint the mural yourself quite easily if you stick to simple designs like bright, bold lines of colour, large clouds, stylized landscapes or favourite cartoon characters.

A hand-painted design costs next to nothing to produce—and even less using left-over paint. If you don't like the results, you can simply paint over it and start again.

Painting a design on a whole wall may be a little adventurous for the beginner and can look overpowering if colours are wrongly chosen, so stick to sections. And just think—children will love anything you do!

If trompe l'oeil frightens you, then try stencils, which are much easier. You can create a false border or dado rail, or highlight a particular area on a plain wall, for example around a picture or mirror. The easiest designs use heavy repeat patterns to create a frieze effect.

You might also be attracted to some of the special-effect painting techniques that have caught the public's imagination once more: stippling, marbling, rag-rolling, sponging and dragging are all very much in fashion now. They are not too difficult to learn, and little mistakes do not show, as the nature of the designs is meant to be irregular. It's a good idea to experiment first on a piece of spare lining paper or hardboard.

Wallpaper

Papers give an all-in-one facelift to a room and create a strong atmosphere instantaneously. They are also better than paint for sub-standard walls, as defects will be less noticeable, especially if lining paper is used underneath.

The choice of wallpapers is absolutely immense, and there are prices to suit all budgets. If you've fallen for a particularly expensive paper but can't afford enough of it for a whole room, don't despair. Check the cheaper ranges first to make sure there is nothing similar—designers often imitate each other.

If you can't find an alternative, then use the paper in small quantities; there are various ways. For example, fix your chosen paper up to dado rail height and paint the remaining section of wall. (If you don't have a dado rail, you can either add an imitation plaster one or strips of wooden beading painted to match the scheme.)

Wallpapers need not be restricted to walls. If the coziness appeals, it can be used across ceilings, doors, panels, cupboards, drawers and other items of furniture. But make sure this doesn't end up looking claustrophobic.

Besides the standard wallcoverings made of paper, there are a number of types which suit specific purposes. They vary in weight and material.

Vinyl papers are water resistant, tough and need a special adhesive. They are ideal for bathrooms and kitchens and other places where a washable surface would be advantageous, such as in a toddler's room.

Anaglypta and *superglypta* papers have specially embossed designs that can be painted over if preferred. They are good for hiding irregular surfaces.

Woodchip papers give an interesting rough look to walls and are available in various textures, from coarse to quite smooth. They are designed to be painted over, and are good for hiding irregularities in the wall or ceiling surface.

Flock is well known for its association with the restaurant trade and its heavy, velvety pattern. But simpler designs are now available, such as simple tiny flock polka dots on a plain background, totally contradicting flock's traditionally 'heavy' image.

Foil and *metallic* papers can create a super-shiny, space-age effect, depending on how much foil is used in the design. Traditional designs are also popular in period homes. They tend to be very expensive, may magnify imperfections and will cause glare if used in very sunny

Below: By carefully using the colours in a wallpaper for furnishings and accessories, you can create a gentle, harmonious effect.

Right: This bedroom ingeniously
combines just two patterns in related
colours for an all-over co-ordinated
effect. The larger-scale pattern is used
for the wallpaper above the dado rail,
curtains, screen, duvet cover,
pillowcases and trim on the roller
blinds, with the smaller-scale pattern
used below the dado rail and for the
valance, fitted sheet and blinds. Even
the rug echoes the pattern. The double
border used round the top of the walls
makes a good substitute for a cornice.

rooms. Take care when using them around light switches and sockets—they are good conductors of electricity. However, they are steam-resistant and will add an exaggerated sense of size and space in a small area. They look particularly good combined with mirror.

Hessian is a very durable wallcovering. It is easy to apply, but apt to fade. Make sure you buy paper-backed hessian especially for walls, as furnishing hessian will shrink once the glue has dried.

Alternative wallcoverings

Fabric is an expensive but undoubtedly effective and warming wallcovering.

Pleated fabric looks extremely sumptuous and softens the harsh edges of a room. Whatever fabric you choose, battens must first be fixed to the wall to ensure an even surface for it to be stretched over. It can then be stapled on to the battens quickly and easily.

Pick a fabric that is fairly crease-resistant, such as a polyester/cotton mix. Sheeting is available in patterns and plains, and glazed chintz has an easy to clean surface, although it is rather expensive. Patterns create a more interesting look than plains, but use designs with a random repeat or you'll have problems matching sections up. One great advantage is that small mistakes will not show.

To cover all the walls of a room with pleated fabric can be very expensive. But you can achieve a similar effect at less cost by using pleated fabric only on certain focal walls, with flat pieces elsewhere.

Wood can be used to create the beautiful wood-panelled effect so seldom found in its original form. At the top end of the market are tongue-and-groove panelling strips which give a beautiful finish and come in all sorts of woods. Veneer is less expensive than solid wood panelling and

is easy to maintain; it suits many styles of furnishing.

Cork and felt make soundproof coverings that insulate well and are fairly easy to apply. They are especially effective in workrooms, studies and playrooms.

Wall tiles are more often chosen for bathrooms and kitchens, although left-over mirror tiles can be used to make an original mirror. To add interest, fix strips of painted wood or dowelling between the tiles and around the outside edges, creating a frame.

Ceiling treatments

Although not vitally important to the room scheme, badly decorated or dilapidated ceilings can let down an

Above: The warm, honey-coloured wood panelling and flooring in this period home provide a perfect background for the dusky pink and smoky blue furnishings.

Above: Tongue-and-groove cladding looks lovely on the ceiling and here complements the picture windows and exposed brickwork very well. Right: With a little artifice, a plain, box-like room can be totally transformed. Here, an ornate wallpaper, divided into panels with decorative wood battens, is combined with a tented ceiling in matching fabric to create a feeling of opulence and luxury.

otherwise beautiful room, so they do warrant some care.

You may simply choose to paint the ceiling in a toning or contrasting colour to the walls. If the ceiling is in poor condition, applying a textured wallpaper before you paint can help (though you must still fill in the cracks first).

Alternatively, you could cover the ceiling with a plain or patterned paper to co-ordinate with walls.

You can actually use colour to change the apparent shape and size of the room. If the ceiling is too high, you can paint it a darker colour, carrying the colour down to the picture rail to accentuate the effect.

To 'raise' the ceiling, paint it a lighter colour than the walls, or apply some sort of reflective surface, such as metallic wallpaper.

Fabric can be applied as successfully to the ceiling as to the walls. A tented ceiling looks most spectacular, especially in a dining room, but you should be extremely adept at diy to attempt it. Swathes of fabric are easier to apply than a tent. Staple the fabric to battens fixed around the edges and across the middle of the ceiling. This gives a soft, boudoir look to a bedroom.

Plaster mouldings around the edges of the ceiling add character to a room and reduce the 'boxy' look some plain rooms have. Alternatively, use stencils to harmonize with the walls or the floor.

Wood beams look really stunning, especially in a house that incorporates them as original features. The wide beams found in old cottages should really be kept natural or black, but the narrow, batten-type false beams found in thirties' houses can be painted in colours to match the rest of the scheme.

Tongue-and-groove panelling is also an effective way to treat ceilings.

If the room is too high and out of proportion, you could build a false ceiling under it. This is often necessary in older houses where large rooms have been divided into smaller ones.

Slatting will create an interesting false ceiling, and is useful for hiding unevenness or ugly light fittings.

False ceilings should clear existing mouldings by a reasonable amount, about 75mm or so.

If the proportions of a room are very badly wrong, you could consider removing the ceiling altogether to expose the joist beams and floorboards of the rooms above. But get professional advice before you go ahead with this, as it is major structural work.

CHAPTER 5

Frame-up

Windows and doors may seem purely functional necessities in your home, yet they play important roles in any room scheme, so you'll want to make the most of them.

Right: Floor to ceiling curtains make a small, insignificant window look much more important. Here pinch pleat heading tape has been used to give a simple, tailored effect. Far right: Soft muslin draped over an additional curtain pole and stapled in place creates an elegant valance for curtains.

The only real source of natural light, windows perform a variety of useful functions in any room—they are your contact with the outside world and may be the most obvious focal point to anyone entering the room. As such, it's important to make the best of them.

Your reasons for choosing a particular window dressing may be one of many—for example, whether or not you want to enhance or hide the view.

Privacy is usually greater at the back of the house than at the front, and back windows may consequently be more casually or openly dressed.

Curtains undoubtedly are an excellent way to dress a window, softening harsh edges and 'framing' it to advantage, but they are not the only option. Blinds have come very much into fashion, and there are lots of styles to choose from.

If neither of these seems suitable for a particular window, you might try one of the other options such as screens, shutters, or even a combination of styles: blinds and curtains together not only look interesting, but also give extra insulation against light and cold.

The bonus about most window dressings is that you can make them yourself—blinds included. There are all sorts of kits around and they're not necessarily difficult; they're also ideal if you're looking for ways to cut the cost.

Whatever your budget, however, never skimp on curtain material. It's better to buy a generous amount of a cheaper fabric than cut down on an expensive one—curtains that lack fullness look mean, even if the fabric used is top quality.

Window dressings can do much to emphasize or heighten the proportion of a window. Tall thin windows will look much wider if the curtain track and curtains are fixed wider than the reveal.

A very poky window can be made to look bigger by using floor-to-ceiling curtains.

Some windows need no dressing at all. Small, circular windows, for example, could probably never be improved, so are best left alone.

All about curtains

Length of curtains is obviously a matter of personal preference, but ideally should be either floor-length or sill-length (allowing about a 7mm gap from the surface to prevent excessive wear). However, pairs of windows of different height can be made to look more uniform if curtains are hung at the same length.

Fabrics and linings

Choice of fabric will depend on a variety of things—the style of the room, your budget, the prearranged scheme and how much or how little light and/or cold you want to keep out.

Traditional fabrics include heavy brocade and velvet, which are perfect for classic styles, while cottons and linens look lighter and more airy. There are also lots of suitable synthetic fabrics. Some furnishing fabrics, especially those for sofas and chairs, are also printed in lighter weights for curtains.

Lining curtains is an excellent way of prolonging their life, and it reduces fading, increases insulation and cuts down the amount of light coming in when curtains are pulled. Lining gives the curtain extra body as well, and, combined with interlining, will make even the cheapest of fabrics hang beautifully. Using the same lining on curtains in different rooms also makes them look more uniform from the outside. There are special metallic linings on the market which will give added insulation.

Of course lining is not essential, and there may be windows where you would

like to achieve a light, sun-filtered effect, such as by French doors overlooking a sunny garden. If sheers and nets are used, they do not need lining.

If you're particularly worried about

place with each curtain, so this may mean ordering more fabric, if there is a large pattern repeat.

Headings

The type of heading tape used will determine the particular style or amount of pleats or gathers at the top of the curtain. Some headings require more fabric than others, so the choice may depend on how much fabric you want to buy. There are three basic types of headings.

Standard gathering tape has drawstrings which, when pulled up, create soft gathers evenly along the length. It uses 1½ to 2 times the track width of fabric and gives the curtain soft, simple gathers. This tape can be used to create cottagey-looking curtains, especially if the tape is positioned about 6cm from the top, forming a frill.

Pinch pleat tape has drawstrings which, when gathered up, form triple pleats with flat sections in between, along the width of the curtain. Some pinch pleat tapes are made with special prongs or hooks instead of drawstrings to create the pleating effect. Pinch pleat heading tape uses 2 to 2½ times the track width of fabric and looks especially good when used on fairly heavy, full-length curtains. It also comes in different widths for lighter fabrics.

Pencil pleat tape, when gathered, creates deep, quite wide, even pleats along the width of the curtain. It requires 2¼ to 2½ times the track width of fabric and looks especially good on lightweight, sheer curtains.

All figures mentioned here are estimations, so check with your local shop when you buy your fabric, especially as amounts may differ from one heading manufacturer to another.

Also available is special lining tape, made so that curtain and lining can be

materials fading, check with the shop or manufacturer—getting a truthful reply may not be easy, but it is worth a try!

If you choose patterned fabric for curtains, the pattern must fall in the same

Above: Lightweight cottons lend themselves well to decorative window dressings and can look extremely pretty with tie-backs in a contrasting colour. Broderie anglaise has been used to create this rather elaborate window dressing. Right: Interesting effects can be obtained with simple drawn thread work, as on this café curtain.

hooked together using separate hooks. This way the lining can be removed for washing or dry cleaning separately from the curtain.

Scalloped headings, generally used for café curtains, look very effective, though they can be quite complicated to make.

Tracks and poles

The weight of the curtain and style of window may determine which type of track you use. Some tracks are made to bend around bay windows, and others to take especially heavy fabrics. Very popular are curtain poles which come in various woods or several metal finishes. The matching rings that go with these are part of the effect, as they show when the curtain is up.

Tracks and poles should, if possible, be at least 45cm wider than the window frame—more if you're trying to give the window an appearance of added width.

Tracks are usually designed to be invisible except when the curtain is pulled open, and then nothing but a neat run of track should show.

Most tracks are made of non-corrosive, strong plastic. There are ultra slim tracks for lightweight curtains, double tracks to take two sets of curtains, ceiling mounted ones for curtains that go right up to ceiling level, and many others.

If you have radiators beneath the window, try to avoid covering them with curtains. Alternatively, there are tracks available with extra long brackets to hold the curtain away from the wall, or you might use a curtain pole with rings so that there is space at the top for the rising warm air to enter the room.

Poles can be bought in many finishes. If you want one in a specific colour but have had no luck finding it, it may be easier to buy an unfinished wooden one and paint it with left-over paint to match the colour scheme.

Pelmets and valances

If you prefer to hide the curtain heading, some sort of pelmet or valance is the solution.

Pelmets can be made of wood, or fabric attached to a board, fitted across the window reveal. They can be shaped in various ways, for example scallops, curves and squares.

Valances are softer than pelmets but serve the same purpose. They usually consist of pleats or gathers of fabric attached to a track or rod, fitted above the window. Valances are also used as headings for four-poster beds.

A more casual approach to creating a valance is to drape or swag fabric over a fixed curtain pole. Once you've an arrangement of fabric that looks fine, you can staple it in place.

Tie-backs

Tie-backs are an excellent way of keeping bulky curtains out of the way during the day, ensuring maximum light from the window. Tie-backs can be made from anything, but are normally matched up in some way with the curtain fabric. Often, they are piped in co-ordinating or contrasting fabric for effect. They are quite easy to make and are attached to the wall by rings.

Borders, braids and trimmings

These can be used to add 'interest' to a curtain, and are usually applied around the inner and bottom edges. There are lots of ready-made braids and trimmings on the market, but simple additions can be made using ribbon or pieces of left-over curtain or upholstery fabric.

Above: This bedroom uses lace curtains to disguise a wardrobe. The three separate panels can be easily drawn to allow access to any part of the wardrobe.

lace is hard to find at a reasonable price, but there are lots of quality modern versions—department stores usually have a wide selection.

Ways with blinds

Blinds were out of fashion for many years as window treatments but have come into their own recently with 'modern' styles, and now with the pretty, voluptuous ruched fabric blinds.

They provide a very practical form of window treatment as they can be drawn right up out of the way simply by pulling a cord, and can be made in any fabric or material, depending on the type of blind. They also have great decorative appeal and manufactured types come in a good variety of colours.

Roller blinds

These are made of treated fabric, are flat when opened and roll up by means of a spring mechanism. They can be used on sloping windows as well as conventional ones, so long as there are channels at either side of the frame for the blind to run up and down.

Many roller blinds can be sponged clean, and ready-made versions offer a choice of trim, shaped bottom edge and pull cord. The range of colours is enormous, and they are bought made to measure. Plain ones are very popular, but most manufacturers also make a variety of patterned blinds, some to match wall-paper manufacturers' designs.

Kits can be bought for those who are a little more adventurous, but the range of ready-made roller blinds is so enormous that it doesn't seem worth the bother—unless you want one in a particular fabric.

Roller blinds are very crisp and clean-looking and go with a variety of house styles. They are useful for combining with other treatments, such as full-length curtains in a Victorian bay window.

Far left: The unusual asymmetrical arrangement of these lace-trimmed net curtains turns the window into a dramatic focal point of the bedroom.
Left: The clean, simple lines of a roller blind are ideal for modern décor.
Above: A lace-trimmed net panel echoes the scalloped edge of this roller blind.

Sheers or nets

Sheers, or nets as they are often called, are most useful for providing privacy without preventing light from entering a room. They can be attached to a rod or pole, at both the top and the bottom, to give taut folds, or they can be attached at the top only for a flowing, graceful look.

There are a variety of special fabrics for use as sheers, but any light-weight material will look good, such as sheer cotton or muslin. Lace is also used and will add the right atmosphere in a particularly pretty or traditional room. Old

They can be used in conjunction with sheers for night-time privacy, then when rolled up during the day, can be hidden by a valance or pelmet.

Roman blinds

These are pulled up by means of a cord, concertina fashion. The cord is threaded through rings attached to the back. When fully raised, roman blinds look rather like a valance. When lowered, the pleats even out and lie flat against the window.

Roman blinds do need to be lined if possible, but they take less fabric than curtains and other types of fabric blinds. They can be made at home but are more complicated than roller blinds.

With their tailored appearance, Roman blinds look good in uncomplicated, modern surroundings. If you're covering a large expanse of glass it's advisable to have more than one blind, as one large one will be difficult to handle.

Festoon blinds

Festoon, ruched or Austrian blinds work on much the same principle as Roman blinds, but instead of pleating, the fabric gathers as it is drawn up to give a full, voluptuous look.

Festoon blinds do not need to be lined and should be made of fairly light fabric. The heading is gathered, and sometimes there is a frill at the bottom edge. They can also be teamed with 'dummy' side curtains, held out of the way with tiebacks.

Kits for making festoon blinds are available, dispensing with the rings that are traditionally sewn on individually.

Rather feminine in effect, they are more often chosen for bedrooms, although they can look very stylish in other rooms if made with material such as plain chintz or taffeta.

Venetian blinds

Venetian blinds are usually made of

metal, but also come in wood or plastic, and are much more resistant to chipping than they used to be. They are available made-to-measure, and some feature slats which are mirrored, while others have tiny pin holes for stylish translucency. There are also designs with plain-coloured slats in a vast choice of hues. You can select from a variety of slat widths, but the ultra-slim type seems to be the most popular.

Venetian blinds are very good for modern settings, where a crisp, clean look is wanted.

Other types

Pleatex blinds are made from strong, treated paper. They come in quite a few colours but parchment colour is also very popular. Permanently pleated, normally

in 2.5cm pleats, Pleatex blinds are cheaper than roller blinds and very strong.

Pinoleum or *matchstick blinds* are good for enhancing the farmhouse or Oriental look. They are made of fine strips of wood woven together with cotton, usually in natural pine. Very inexpensive, they are a good way of

covering large expanses of glass. They look better on their own rather than with other forms of window treatment.

Vertical blinds are made from vertical strips of wood, silk or canvas and are usually floor-to-ceiling in length. They draw horizontally, rather like a curtain. These blinds can also be used successfully as a screen to divide rooms up temporarily. They tend to be expensive but now come in a range of patterns as well as plains.

Alternative treatments

If you want something a little more continental, louvre and other types of shutters can be tailor-made to fit any size window. However, heat retention and insulation must be reasonable to use such a window treatment on its own.

Fitted to open concertina-fashion, shutters will not take up room space when open, and they can be painted or stained to match your colour scheme.

Windows with a deep reveal look good with shutters fitted on the frame, possibly with another treatment on the outside of the reveal (such as full-length curtains or a blind of some kind).

If you have original shutters, avoid

Facing page and this page: Modern blinds are practical, cheap, attractive and versatile. Roller blinds (facing page, left) are the perfect solution for an awkward window, even one in the roof, where it is fixed upside down. Roman blinds (facing page, right) are pulled up concertina-fashion, giving a modern, tailored effect. Venetian blinds (this page, left) allow you to control the amount of light you let into the room, simply by adjusting the metal, wooden or plastic slats. Pleatex blinds (this page, centre) have gained in popularity, as they are relatively cheap. Made from strong, permanently pleated paper, they come in a choice of colours. Pinoleum blinds (this page, right) are used to filter rather than block the light; they are fairly inexpensive but can be awkward to operate.

removing them for the sake of changing the window style. Instead, think of ways of incorporating them to harmonize with the room scheme.

An inexpensive screen can be made using garden trellis, painted in a co-ordinating colour. Alternatively, you can simply stand a jointed screen in front of the window at nights.

If it's only the bottom half of the window you want to screen off from the outside world, café curtains or a roller blind fixed halfway down the frame is ideal.

Shutters are good for dining rooms and studies where you want an informal dressing that will not detract from the atmosphere.

Ideas for windows

There's no 'right' or 'wrong' way to dress a window, but here are a few ideas for dealing with common styles of window.

Sash windows look good with roller blinds as they emphasize the shape of the window. Georgian sashes which have retained their original shutters may need no other treatment unless they're particularly draughty. As these windows tend to be fairly large, often with tiny sills, floor-length curtains look elegant.

Bay windows are a beautiful feature in any house. By using special flexible tracks, you can treat the whole bay with one run of floor-length curtains. If there's little space at the top of the window, the track can be ceiling-mounted.

Sheers at bay windows can also be used as a complete curtain, giving unity. Since bay space is often under-utilized, a window seat would be a stylish addition. In this case, sill-length curtains are ideal.

If you're fixing blinds to a bay, each window should have a separate one.

Casement windows benefit from any type of blind, although festoon blinds look particularly attractive. If the reveal is deep, fix sill-length curtains inside the frame, or ·outside using a decorative curtain pole.

Windows in pairs look especially good if they're treated as one (particularly if they're in proportion with each other), with curtains on either side, held back during the day with tie-backs. Alternatively, matching blinds will make them into a focal point.

Picture windows are designed to let in a great deal of light, and this feature should be enhanced as much as possible. Choose curtain tracks or poles that extend far enough beyond the reveal to allow curtains to be drawn right back from the window. Crisp blinds, such as Venetians, and even shutters, look good with these modern windows.

French windows usually need to be accessible from a garden or patio, so shutters, vertical blinds or full-length curtains which pull all the way back are best. This is one place where unlined curtains may be preferable. As French windows are not usually overlooked, sheers or nets are not in general necessary.

Arched, semicircular and round windows are best left alone unless privacy is a problem. If it is, either fit them with frosted glass, or use café curtains so that the shaped top is unaffected.

Options for doors

Don't imagine that the only option for doors is to paint them in a single colour to match the rest of the room. Of course, this is a very acceptable way of creating stylish simplicity, but if you would like to try something a little different, there are lots of ways to perk up a door.

If you're lucky and have panelled doors, you can paint the panels in different colours or pick out the indents in one colour.

You could try painting a door with a design that matches something in a nearby picture—this might make a very interesting feature for a children's room.

Doors come in all shapes and sizes, and sometimes it might be worth replacing

Far left: Shutters create a cozy, intimate atmosphere and accentuate a nicely shaped window. Left above and below: Panelled doors (below) look very smart painted in one solid colour. Alternatively, you can paint the panels a different shade, or pick out just the indents in a contrasting colour as on these wardrobe doors (above).

Above and above right: Louvre doors between a living room and dining room are perfect for entertaining, as they can be partially or completely closed for an intimate dinner party, or opened to create a large, open-plan area for a party.

one that you consider boring and un-imaginative, or not suited to the style of the house. There are many replacement doors that can be bought in standard sizes or custom-made. They may be wood, aluminium or glazed; solid or hollow; panelled, louvred, carved, etched or plain. Do ensure that whatever you choose will fit in with the rest of the décor. If you have an older house, a salvage company may have a selection of doors well suited to the period of the house.

If doors are really draughty, a door curtain will help. This can be made of a fabric to match the windows and should be lined for double insulation. (Draught excluders are important, too, of course.)

Doors you dispense with can be made use of too—saw them in half lengthwise, add hinges and you've a useful screen!

Choosing doors

Panelled doors are very attractive because of their versatility. They can be painted or stained, or rubbed down and left natural—whatever suits you.

Panelled doors are made up of thick surrounds into which four or more thinner panels are set. Sometimes mouldings are added for detail, which can in themselves be picked out with paint for a more interesting effect.

If draughts are not a problem, louvred doors are interesting replacements. They might be used, for example, as a bedroom door, between a living room and dining room or between a bedroom and en suite bathroom. Louvre panels can be fitted to existing doors if draughts are a problem

but genuine louvres are more authentic-looking.

Glass doors come in many styles. Those with frosted glass let in light while protecting privacy, and they avoid the disconcerting reflections that clear glass gives. Of course care must be taken with glass anywhere in the home, especially with children around, and doors are no exception. Safety glass is less likely to shatter than ordinary glass, so try to use this where possible.

Stable doors are divided into two so that the top half can be opened on its own, making a useful hatch between a dining room and a kitchen.

Mirrored doors are useful but are best restricted to bedrooms to avoid startling people with their own reflections.

Floor-to-ceiling doors can enhance and make much of a large, old house.

Doors can be decorated with as many materials as walls—fabric, paper, borders, stencils, as well as plain old paint. If you've used a border around a room, why not continue it on to the doors? Alternatively, make a feature of a door by using a border all around the frame, making sure you mitre the corners for neatness.

Cork is good for covering doors, especially in a bedroom or study, as it can be used as a pinboard.

If doors have unattractive accessories, change them. Door furniture can be bought in many styles and by simply replacing the door knobs, adding stylish finger plates, and so on, you can add a lot of character. Plastic handles can be bought for children's rooms, ornate brass pieces for a living room. The choice is large: door furniture is available in china, glass, bronze, brass, acrylic, wood, and plastic.

Doors can be re-hung to open out-wards if space is a problem, or replaced with sliding models.

CHAPTER 6

First impressions

Often forgotten until the last minute in decoration schemes,
the hall, stairs and landing are nevertheless important, and
need to be both welcoming and functional.

Right: In some halls a narrow bit of otherwise wasted space can be converted into a downstairs cloakroom. If the ceiling is fairly high, a useful storage cupboard can be fitted above the room without the space being missed. Using the same colour scheme as in the hall makes the cloakroom as unobtrusive as possible.

The hall is the very first area guests will see upon entering and may determine their opinion of the rest of the house—so careful planning is important.

Because guests spend relatively little time in these areas, it is possible to be a little more dramatic here than elsewhere. If, however, a number of rooms are visible from a hall, its scheme should not be too noticeably different.

A décor that seems exciting and vibrant to somebody who only sees it once a month may well become jarring to the people who have to live with it.

Halls, stairs and landings can be difficult areas to organize, partly due to their shape, which is often very awkward, and partly to the requirement of being extremely practical as well as pleasing to the eye.

Like other areas, halls and landings should have a clearly defined traffic route. There should be no hazardous obstacles to fall over or slippery flooring to slide along. Lighting is important too, enabling everyone to get from one area to another without stumbling in the dark.

How much you can get out of a hall may depend on how big it is. If there's a lot of wasted space at one end, this can be turned into a downstairs cloakroom or a cupboard of some kind. Equally, if there's lots of space under the stairs, this can be utilized (see page 71).

A certain amount of furniture is needed in a hall, unless you're planning to hang everything on the wall. The items you may need are: a shelf or table for telephone, notepads, directories; an umbrella stand; a shoe-rack and a coatstand or cupboard. Some of these may be superfluous to your own needs.

Lighting the way

Lack of light is often a problem in halls and landings, especially if there is nowhere for natural light to enter. Thus the only source may be artificial lighting, and usually from just one central pendant fitting. This could be quite inadequate, and you may need extra sources by the telephone, front door and mirror and under the stairs.

Staircases must be well lit for safety. There should be sufficient two-way switches for the lights to be turned on whichever direction you're going. It is ideal to have a system that connects at each level, from the hall upwards, so that there is always a switch to illuminate the next storey up. The light at the top of the stairs should be stronger than that below, so that the steps themselves are clearly visible.

One way to add space as well as light to a hall or landing is to remove a wall, or part of one, of an adjoining room. If a hall serves no real purpose as a room in its own right, you might benefit from having an open-plan entry or open-plan archway leading to the living room or kitchen. To reduce heat loss in this situation, it would be wise to hang an extra-heavy or specially insulated curtain at the front door.

Knocking down any internal wall, or even part of a wall, must be thought out carefully, as some alteration work is more dangerous and complicated than it seems. You should always consult an architect or builder about safety and building regulations.

Less drastic steps would be to install glass panels above a door, or into a section of a solid internal door or front door. For privacy, for example in a bedroom door, the glass could be frosted.

Artificial light will have to be well thought out. Bulbs under 100 watts will give out a dull, dreary glow, not sufficient for a hall, so choose pendant lights that will take a high wattage. You can supplement this using spotlights or

downlighters—but they ought to be used to illuminate the passageways, and not just for decorative effect.

Mirrors can be used effectively to increase light. If a whole wall of mirror in a hall seems too expensive, a selection of wall-hung mirrors or strips of miniature mirror tiles will do the trick.

Wall coverings

Whatever you put on the walls, remember that these are the areas most

Above: Painting the dado to contrast with the rest of the walls makes this hall look less long and narrow.

likely to get dirty, especially if you have small children, so choose something spongable or washable. If you choose paint, vinyl silk is ideal; gloss provides a washable surface, but does tend to show up irregularities in the surface.

Any wallpaper that is water-resistant or can be sponged is ideal. Hessian is a fairly practical covering as it is tough and hardwearing, and it comes in lots of colours. It can also be painted over later, should you change the scheme.

Treat any doors that lead off a hall or landing as part of that area and decorate them in accordance with the scheme. Don't just play safe, however; there are as many options open to this side of doors as any other. You can add fun details to bedroom doors, for example, by personalizing them with hand-painted designs.

Stair walls may seem hopelessly boring areas with little decorative choice, but this is certainly not the case. There is usually a larger expanse of wall than anywhere else. It can be the perfect place to display all the pictures, family portraits, and so on, that won't fit elsewhere. You can also add dado rails or borders on the stair wall to lead the eye upwards.

As in any area, darkish colours will make it look smaller, whereas light ones increase size and reflect light. Be careful, however, of using pastel colours to cheer up these areas. If lighting is poor, these tones can end up simply looking grey, so it might be better to go for something bold and warm. Of course the alternative is to improve the lighting!

If ceilings are dark and imposing, or too high or low, you can alter their appearance in a variety of ways using lighter and darker paints (see page 42).

Halls, stairs and landings are ideally suited to geometric and angular patterned wallpaper. Whatever you use, however, try to continue your choice of decoration for the hall into the stair and landing areas—sudden changes from one to the other will look distinctly uncomfortable.

Combined with all this, you must take into account the décor of the rooms leading off these areas. To go from one extreme to another may be too much of a shock after a while, especially in a small house. Work out how each area can be co-ordinated—possibly by using a basic colour scheme and picking out different tones from it for different levels.

Suitable flooring

Halls, stairs and landings are the areas throughout the house which will take most wear, so whatever goes on the floor must be hard-wearing and durable. Carpet, matting, linoleum, vinyl, treated wood, quarry tiles and carpet tiles are all good choices, although some are obviously more suited to the hall than the stairs or landing.

If you are using carpet, it must be a good-quality, hard-wearing one or it will become thin and patchy after a while. A good carpet retailer will advise you if you're not sure. Don't use rugs unless they are very heavy and fitted with a non-slip underlay.

Whatever the hall floor is covered with, the stairs are best carpeted to cut down on noise and prevent slipping. This can be either wall-to-wall or strip carpet. If you choose the latter, you'll have to decide what you're going to do with the borders on either side of the strip. They can be painted to match the scheme or stained in a toning colour. If you want patterned carpet for the stairs, choose one with a random or small repeat; large repeat patterns will get lost between the treads and just look odd and imbalanced.

Unless you're expert, you should use a professional carpet fitter for stairs. It is especially important that the carpet is stretched and fitted properly to pre-vent accidents caused by buckling and excessive wear.

Make sure you have a good-sized mat at the front door—a small one will be inadequate and look out of proportion.

Utilizing space

Entrance halls and landings are often under-utilized. For example, they may take some of the load off other rooms by providing extra storage space, and there may be space in a hall to put shelves for plants, books or ornaments. A seemingly useless corner may be just right for a display table that cannot be fitted elsewhere. A small round table covered with a pretty cloth makes the ideal spot for an extra lamp or treasured portrait collection.

If the hall is very small or narrow, there are certain ways to save space. For example, instead of having a telephone on a table, install a wall-mounted model. Keep other items out of the way by putting up a mass of strong hooks for coats, umbrellas, even telephone directories (using strong loops of cord to hold them up).

Plants can be used to brighten up these areas: potted ones in halls and landings, and hanging plants above the stairs.

Some halls and landings are spacious enough to be used for other purposes, either temporarily or permanently. A hall, for example, that's divided from a living room by an archway or semi-open plan system, might be used as a dining area or a study.

A drop-down table can be wall-fixed in a closed-in hallway, making a temporary work area. Pinboards look good in the hall, and are useful for keeping track of letters, taxi numbers, postcards, memos.

Large landings with suitable safety gates at the top of the stairs might easily become play areas for the children.

Handrails are often ignored, yet these can be painted in exciting colours or in toning shades.

Make a feature of any window in a hall or landing. Those you get at the top of stairwells are often quite large and would benefit from special treatment.

Left: Strip carpet in a small pattern is perfect for a traditional style of décor. Below: This ingenious coat rack is not only handy, but it helps to create a separate entrance area in an open-plan hall and living room.

CHAPTER 7

All change

Wherever you live, there's always something you can do to improve or make the most of your home, whatever its limitations may be.

The minute you enter your home, whether it be a rented flat, a new house or an established family home, it should mean something to you. After all, it is the area where you can be yourself most and where you expect to relax in surroundings chosen by you and stamped with your own individuality.

Your budget and personal circumstances may dictate how you plan interior design. But every home will have certain characteristics: some of these you may have to resign yourself to, while others can be utilized to the full.

Space stretching

Have you really looked around you? There may well be corners, possibilities, characteristics that you either didn't know were there or simply hadn't noticed before.

Before you start knocking down walls or adding new rooms, decide whether you can make more of what you've got by changing the functions of existing rooms. Only when you've exhausted such possibilities should you start to build or extend.

Rooms can be combined for greater convenience, especially in older houses: for example, hall and living room; kitchen and dining room; wc and bathroom. Some internal walls may be load-bearing, however, so be sure to find out which they are first.

Another alternative is to divide large rooms into separate areas, making better use of available space. Partitions do not need to be expensive or permanent. A tall bookcase works well, for instance, and provides added storage facilities as well as being accessible from both sides. A light, ceiling-hung blind is an even simpler partition—which is equally easily dispensed with.

Consider whether you have utilized all the areas where storage can be incorpor-ated without detracting from the layout of the rooms. Good ready-made storage units can be expensive, so look around at the areas where it can be built in—for example, a false ceiling in a tall hall can be used to store suitcases. Build it in two sections so that there is accessible space in the middle.

The space above a door is a good area for one or two shelves, ideal for storing little-used items. The backs of cupboards are usually left free, whereas the addition of a number of hooks will make them into a useful extra storage space.

Rented flats

Interior design doesn't have to be restricted to home owners. Just because you rent doesn't mean that you don't care about the circumstances in which you live.

Obviously, it may not be worth spending lots of money on something you might leave within a short space of

Below left: Cupboards on each side of a door, with a shelf along the top, create valuable extra storage space. Below right: The area inside a bay window is often the least-used part of a room. This design makes the best use of the available space with a built-in pine unit which incorporates seating, display shelves and an enclosed cupboard.

time, but you can make small and relatively cheap improvements that will make life more comfortable and pleasant.

There may be certain restrictions imposed by the landlord. There is usually more licence to adapt and/or decorate unfurnished accommodation than furnished.

Brightening it up

The first step is to make sure that every surface is as clean as you can get it. What may seem like a dirty-coloured wall can look a million times better for a good scrub.

A tin of paint goes a long way, and it really is the cheapest decoration medium. It depends on individual circumstances as to whether you will be allowed to use paint, so it's wise to check with the landlord first.

Have all your suggestions at hand, including paint samples, so that he/she can see exactly what you plan to do. Most landlords won't mind at all if you want to decorate, as long as what you want to do is 'reasonable'. After all, it saves them the time and money it would cost to employ decorators.

If you can't afford a lot of paint, use a small amount to highlight areas like window frames, skirting boards and picture rails, or just paint one area like the ceiling.

Personal touches

There are other additions you can make as well, which will be temporary—useful for when you move on.

If the carpet is in bad condition or in a horrible design, cover it with as many rugs as you can afford. They don't have to be expensive; in fact, if you're adept with your hands, you can make some yourself. The great thing about rugs is that they'll always be useful, wherever you happen to be living.

Small pieces of provided furniture and accessories can be hidden away as much as possible in cupboards and corners, leaving space for you to add your own.

Walls can be disguised in a variety of ways. Pictures in quantity look good, but avoid putting them up with sticky substances—this not only looks messy, but leaves nasty marks on the wall after a period of time. Most landlords would rather you left the tiny holes created by proper picture nails. Plastic poster hangers that slip on to the poster at the top and bottom edges are quite cheap and make them hang better. If you've a picture rail, you can use this to hang all pictures from, without making holes in the wall.

Clip-on frames are inexpensive and come in various sizes, from postcard upwards. They provide instant, cheap framing for those who can't afford proper framing prices. Collections of old or interesting postcards look especially good in these.

Cover-up job

Fabric can be an inexpensive way to cover up ugly walls. Hang it using lengths of thin wire, elastic or special curtain wires, threaded through a channel sewn along the top edge of the fabric. This can then be attached to the wall using picture nails or small tacks at each end and, if needed, in the middle. Butter muslin and other light fabrics are very cheap and give a soft, translucent look to walls.

These fabrics can also be used as curtains. If you remove original curtains, however, take care of the old ones—you will have to put them back when you leave. Pinoleum blinds are cheap alternatives to window dressings and can be cut later to fit smaller windows. If you can get hold of some broom handles, they can be used as an alternative to proper

curtain poles, which can cost a lot of money.

Ugly furniture such as tables, chairs and sofas can be easily disguised by draping it with fabric.

Lighting ideas

Lighting is another easily changed provision. If you have been provided with a central pendant fitting that you don't like, replace it with a cheap, paper globe design. If it's simply in the wrong place, extend the flex, screw a hook into the ceiling above where you want it to shine and loop the flex over the hook.

Good quality lamps and light fittings are a worthwhile buy. Cheap practical ones are good alternatives if money is short, but if you also invest in something a little more luxurious, it will always look good and be useful later on. Clip-on spotlights don't cost much and can be extremely useful, especially if you want to highlight a particular plant or corner, or just need a well-lit area in which to study.

Furniture and accessories

Screens are easy to make and will hide ugly corners very well. They can be constructed from most solid materials. Old doors, for example, are suitable, as are large pieces of cheap hardboard, available from any local timber merchant. Paint them and then, if desired, add your own stencilled and painted motifs.

If you need furniture of any kind, hunt around auction rooms and second-hand shops—pieces can still be found. As long as they're practical and sound it doesn't matter how tatty they are. They can be restored, painted, stencilled, sprayed, and so on to give an individual touch.

Big, squashy floor cushions provide cheap additional seating and can be made quite easily.

Below: To separate the living area and kitchen in an open-plan room, a screen made from garden trellis, with indoor plants climbing up it, is both attractive and functional. Opposite: Squeezing the bedroom, bathroom and living room together is easier if you create a built-in platform. Here, a mini-bathroom fits neatly under a raised bed.

Plants brighten up any room and are worthwhile investments if you keep them in good condition. Large potted palms look luxurious, but there are lots of inexpensive smaller plants available which add a lot to a room.

If you've lots of books to store, you can make bookshelves from strips of wood or glass, fixed up with brackets. A floor-standing version can be made with piled-up bricks, as long as they're fairly clean.

One-room living

The biggest problem in one-room living is obviously lack of space, as anyone who has lived in such accommodation knows.

Not only does this usually mean a cramped sort of lifestyle, but the close vicinity of the kitchen area provides unwanted odours whenever cooking has taken place.

The confinement is probably the most irritating and depressing element of one-room living. There may well be a separate bathroom, but all other functions have to take place in the one area. Theoretically, the room should be big enough to take all this into account, but this is not always the case.

Functions within the room fall into two categories which in some way should be divided—sleeping/living and cooking/eating.

If you're actually planning this type of accommodation for somebody in particular, as part of your house (a special area for teenagers, for example, or perhaps a granny flat), you will have a 'shell' from which you can make the best possible arrangements. If on the other hand you already live in a one-room flat, you must adapt whatever you have.

Rooms which are L-shaped or T-shaped have more potential than those that are square or rectangular, as certain functions are naturally separated from others by the shape of the room.

Above and right: A living/dining room can double as a bedroom if you include a sofa-bed and an extending table which tidies away when not required.

If areas need separating, particular items of furniture may suffice as room dividers. A run of either high or low bookshelves with open shelving is ideal, and accessible from both sides. Screens of various types make great dividers, too, and they can be folded up and propped against a wall when they're not needed.

Living and sleeping in one room

One way of fitting more into a small area is by building the various functional areas on a stepped arrangement. Think about building the bed on a platform of some kind, leaving the area below for living, dining or even storage. This is especially feasible in high-ceilinged rooms.

Or you could choose the type of bed that can be made into a sofa during the day. This could be either an ordinary bed, which you cover with cushions, or a sofa bed specially for the purpose. If you choose a sofa bed, buy the best you can afford. For such permanent use as this, you'll want something that both looks good and feels comfortable whether you are sitting or sleeping on it.

Alternatively, two single beds can be divided into an L-shaped sofa, pushed into a corner during the day, and clipped together at night. A bed can also be kept in a corner and sectioned off by a curtain, blind, screen or partition of some kind.

You may prefer the type of bed that can be lifted and stowed out of the way, complete with bedlinen, in a cupboard style enclosure. These come in single and double bed versions and are great for dispensing with sleeping arrangements entirely during the day. However, do take into account the quality of the bed, and never sacrifice comfort for convenience.

Other furniture should be light, flexible and at a minimum. Glass-topped tables seem to take up less space than

Left and below: An alternative to a sofa-bed is a fold-away bed, which tucks neatly into a cupboard, or behind a curtain in an alcove, during the day.

Below: If it suits your lifestyle, one open-plan room combining living room, dining area, hall and kitchen creates a light, airy, spacious effect. Right: Here's an ingenious alternative to a roller blind for a roof window in a loft conversion—curtains tucked behind a second curtain pole along the bottom.

solid ones and a couple of folding chairs are worth investing in.

Storage needs for the living/sleeping area are for bedding, clothes, crockery, books, records, personal papers and other possessions. Keep these to a minimum if you possibly can, as you won't have much space for hoarding.

A cupboard in an alcove or recess is ideal for storing clothes. Organize the interior properly—a rail for hanging clothes, and a selection of baskets, drawers and shelves for shoes, socks, underwear, and so on.

Other solutions are to fit a rail across an alcove and hide it with a curtain or blind, or buy a secondhand clothes rail which can either be hidden in the same way or left freestanding in a corner.

Building a wall-length, walk-in cupboard may mean sacrificing some of the floor space, but it is ideal for storing absolutely everything. You may have less space for walking around in but you'll have a neat line of storage and little clutter elsewhere.

One-room kitchen areas

The kitchen area may need to be hidden most of the time, as it can be quite an eyesore. A partition of some kind is the best solution.

A double-sided room divider is ideal, since you can store books and living needs on one side and appliances, tools and kitchen items on the other.

Try to keep equipment to a minimum. Space is probably already limited, so you don't want to clutter what you have with gadgets and useless items.

An extractor fan to keep cooking odours and steam at a minimum is a valuable addition in this area, while a cooker hood will deal with steam and odours even more effectively.

Consider how easy it will be to run the necessary services—water, drainage, electricity—to the room. You will probably have to install more power points and possibly a cooker point. If you're in doubt about any of this, get expert advice before starting any major work and check on local building regulations.

Extensions and conversions

You may consider some sort of extension or conversion to make more of your house.

Any conversion or extension is subject to certain building regulations. Before you start, inquire about local building regulations which might affect your

Right: With the right decorative treatment, the sloping walls in a loft conversion can be turned into an attractive feature which adds to the charm of the room.

plans, and find out whether you will need planning permission for them. It might be a good idea to chat to an architect or surveyor first and find out what problems you are likely to encounter, thus making yourself fully prepared.

Converting the loft

The attic or loft is the area most commonly extended into. Most houses with sloping roofs have adequate space that can be utilized. If it is not possible to do a full-scale room conversion, it may still provide facilities for extra storage space, helping to take the load off other rooms in the house.

What the space can be used for will depend on the size. Possibilities include an extra bedroom, a playroom, a study, a sewing room or simply a well-organized store that may even be used as a wardrobe, if it is close to a bedroom.

If you want to make the loft into a usable room, it should be high enough to stand up in. There are regulations concerning headroom which differ from place to place. In general you will need a minimum height of 2.3 metres over at least half of the floor area.

If you're using the area as a store, the amount of access needed will depend on what you are storing. It will, for example, be more important if you're storing bulk-buy foods for all-year-round use than if you're leaving seasonal things like skis and garden furniture there.

Avoid putting too much weight on one joist. They are not designed to take great loads individually, and existing loft joists are rarely meant to carry the weight of a proper floor, so they may have to be strengthened.

Even if you're not converting the loft but still use it quite often, it is a good idea to cover the joists with some form of solid flooring to avoid accidentally putting your feet between them and through the ceiling below. Sheets of chipboard will do —lay them side by side across the joists to prevent dirt or damage to any insulation between the joists.

You must ensure that there is a light switch sited on the floor below the loft to avoid stumbling about in the dark when gaining access.

You will need some form of ladder or step arrangment to reach the loft. If

you're converting it into a useful room, such as a bedroom, you may want to build a proper staircase. In any circumstances, it is better to fit a pull-down, proprietary loft ladder than to use one that's usually kept elsewhere.

Whatever the loft's being used for, check that there are no holes in the roof and that the whole area is watertight.

Although you can do a certain amount of structural work in this area yourself, it is best to call in some sort of specialist advice before you begin.

If there isn't one already, you will probably have to install a window. Choose a style in keeping with the other windows of the house; while the interior does not need to harmonize with other parts of the house, the exterior should.

In terms of décor, you can either make a feature of the sloping walls by using a stronger colour or bolder pattern, or play them down by decorating walls and ceiling in the same neutral shade. If the loft is fairly large, emphasizing the walls will be quite effective, but in a smaller or irregularly shaped loft, this will make the area look cramped. If the room has unusual angles, avoid large patterns, which detract from the charm of the shape and tend to overwhelm the room. Finally, when selecting a colour scheme, take into account the amount of light the room receives.

Basement conversion

The main problem with converting basements or cellars is usually the lack of light, access and headroom. While it may take a lot of planning to turn a dead area like an unused basement into a success, it can be well worth the effort. A well planned basement or cellar may be turned into a variety of useful things, such as a playroom, a study, a living room, or even a bedsit for younger members or elderly relatives.

Make sure the basement has a sufficient damp-proof course. If not, you should check what steps you need to take in order to render it completely damp-free. This applies to floors as much as to walls; in fact, defective and extremely damp floors are best replaced.

If light is a problem, you may have to extend available windows or cut new ones. Light may be blocked by obstacles outside windows, such as bushes, sloping banks or trees, and these can either be cut back or removed.

Well-planned artificial light is important—the greater the impression of natural light the better. Fluorescent lighting is a good source, but is best hidden around window frames or similar places. If headroom is restricted, wall and spotlights are much better than pendant fittings.

Extending the heating system into the basement area may not be too much of a problem if the boiler is already located in this part of a house. If it isn't, then individual heaters, such as gas or electric fires, or storage heaters may be the answer.

Colour schemes may have to compensate for the lack of natural light, so treat this area like any other with this problem (see page 10).

Adding on

If you own your property, you may have areas of land around the house that are large enough to build some sort of extension on. Building regulations apply here too, and you may also need planning permission. This will take into account a number of things, among them whether or not your extension in any way disturbs your neighbours.

You would be best advised to consult a solicitor or surveyor to talk over your needs. Whatever you plan, try to keep to the style of the original house as far as possible. Check there are no covenants in the title deeds of your house to restrict what you can build.

Decide very carefully what the extension is going to be used for. Only then can you determine what kind of plumbing, electrical and other needs should be taken into account.

There are different ways to go about building an extension, once you've made up your mind.

Package kits are for those who want to get into diy. However, they are not really appropriate for rooms that are going to be used all year round, as they are not particularly sturdy and they need regular maintenance. A package kit might be best used for a sun-room type extension.

Architects will not only help you design your extension, but, if you want, will carry the operation through to the end: taking quotations from builders, supervising the building, checking accounts and so on. Of course this can be expensive.

Specialist firms who deal only in extensions will offer the same sort of complete service. They are cheaper than architects in general, but their main disadvantage is that they usually have a limited number of designs.

Under the stairs

Unless it is the entrance to a basement, the area under the stairs is usually large enough to be put to some use; in fact, it may already be a cupboard of some kind. On the other hand, it might simply be an open space that you hadn't considered for really practical use before.

Older houses usually have quite a large space under the stairs, which is easily converted into an additional 'room' such as a workroom, a downstairs cloakroom, a sewing area, a utility area, or even a darkroom if your hobbies include photography.

Opening up the space is quite a simple operation. Remove the side panelling and door (if there is one). Check the quality of the wood on the underside of the steps and, if it is in bad condition, enclose it with a false 'ceiling' of hardboard or tongue-and-groove panels. Uneven walls should be replastered or panelled over.

It is best to use the same decoration in this space as the hall, to give a sense of continuity. Extra power sockets can be installed relatively simply, especially if the house is wired on the ring main system—check with an electrician if in doubt.

Putting up shelves will be relatively easy, and wood can be cut to fit any awkward shapes, like the sloping underside of the stairs.

Make a temporary door in front of the space by putting up a blind or louvred doors, or a curtain to match the scheme.

If you are going to make this area into a

Far left: With clever conversion and light, cozy decoration, a loft can be an excellent place to site a second living room. Left: A house with a disused cellar or basement can be extended downwards. The job may be easier than converting a loft or building an extension.

darkroom, you'll obviously have to put up a more permanent type of entrance, checking that there are no cracks where light can enter and spoil expensive photographic papers.

Both a darkroom and a downstairs cloakroom need some sort of plumbing and ventilation—you should check regulations concerning these before you start planning.

A small handbasin and a wc with a narrow cistern are ideal for a cloakroom in a confined space. But if building regulations prevent you from installing a wc, you may still be able to put in a useful handbasin, and use the remaining space for coats and shoes.

If the understair area is part of a living room, treat it as an alcove and fill it with a shelving system to hold books, stereo, tv and so on. This will leave the rest of the room free from clutter.

Functional spare rooms

A spare room is an asset in any home, but is quite often wasted. Even if it is already used as a guest room, it could be combined with another function to make practical use of the space when you don't have guests staying.

There's no reason why the room should not take on two or three functions —a guest room when need be and an extra amenity to take some of the load off the rest of the house at other times.

Think about how you could best use an extra room, then decide how it can be changed to fulfil these needs. At this stage, you will not want to spend too much money, but rather change what is available into something useful. It could, for example, become a sewing room, an office or a playroom.

Make a list of all the equipment and furniture that you're going to need in the room, and draw up a plan to see how these things will fit.

Guest necessities can be slotted around this. Think of various ways to make the bed as unobtrusive as possible. A sofa bed, for example, is quite adequate, or you could try a folding design that will slip out of the way under a work desk.

Bedding can be stored in one section of a shelving unit or chest, with the remaining space kept for working necessities.

Try to keep as much of the floor as free as possible, and use the walls wherever you can. A worktop can be either fixed so that it flaps down from the wall, or incorporated into a cupboard or wardrobe.

Whatever purpose you're putting the room to, storage bins, baskets and trays will come in useful. The bins will keep larger items out of the way, and baskets and trays can be wall mounted.

CHAPTER 8

Solid investments

Choosing furniture to your own preferences is like putting a
stamp of independence on a room. The most important thing
is that you are happy with your choice.

Choosing furniture is not simply a matter of spending money. Before you even contemplate splashing out large amounts of cash, you must assess what you really do need and whether you can make certain 'compromises' until you can afford luxuries.

What you buy will depend on whether you are either starting from scratch or already have certain pieces that you want to retain or renovate in some way.

Most people accumulate far too much furniture. Even so, it can be heartbreaking to part with anything, especially if it has sentimental or nostalgic value.

If you have an area where pieces of furniture can be stored, use it to the full. Attics are rarely organized carefully enough, and a little planning may mean you can store all redundant furniture without having to actually throw it out or sell it. Some pieces might find new homes in different rooms than those originally planned. For example, old armchairs can be great assets in bedrooms.

Basic planning

Make a comprehensive list of what you will *need* for each room; do not include pieces you want simply for their aesthetic value.

There are certain basics everyone needs: seating and storage in the living room, table and chairs in the dining area, beds and storage in the bedrooms, possibly a table in the hall and so on. Kitchens and bathrooms have their obvious requirements which may depend on the size and space available.

Other necessities depend on circumstances—how big rooms are, whether or not you have spare rooms or a study, how much built-in storage you already have, whether you live in a house or a tiny bedsit.

If you've certain styles, ranges and renovations in mind, assess how much

they all will cost or how much you want to spend on each, and add this to your list. Add up the total and see how it fares with your budget. If it's too much, examine the list to see where you can make cuts. If it's too little (which is less likely!) you have leeway to include luxuries.

Once you've achieved a practical list that comes within your budget, you can incorporate these theoretical pieces into your room plan (see page 14).

Personal style

There is no such thing as good or bad taste, only individual preferences. Never be swayed by anyone if you really want something in particular—although you may have to be pretty thick-skinned sometimes!

The most important thing is for you to be happy with your choice—and to remain that way. Obviously, you would not want to pick something that you'll grow tired of in a few years' time. This can occur if you choose especially outrageous designs.

Having confidence and knowing what you like will help enormously when you are picking furniture. But you must also consider the scheme, the proportion of the room against the furniture, and certain practicalities such as whether or not you have children and how old they are.

Like everything in home design, it is helpful to look around you and see how things work together in other people's homes and in magazine photographs.

Distinguish between personal style and 'generic' style—the latter being a design that has grown out of a certain period or monarchy, such as 50s, 60s, Regency, Tudor, and so on. If you want to stick to a certain generic style, go ahead and do so, but you may find that you tire of its insistent atmosphere after a while. On

the other hand, a bland, undemanding décor, though safe, won't arouse much enthusiasm.

Pieces of furniture in different styles often blend together well, although some obviously do so better than others.

Of course you will probably not want to dispense with a valuable item that

Above: Dressers come in many styles and are a perfect place for displaying treasured collections of plates, china and nick-nacks.

Right: Here's an interesting alternative to the three-piece suite—a sofa, an armchair in the same style but co-ordinating fabric, and a wing chair in fabric to match the other chair.

was inherited from, perhaps, a distant relation, but you could pick other pieces to blend with it, without reducing comfort. If you already collect such pieces, you need no help—you will know enough about antiques to design your own schemes over and over again.

Sofas and armchairs

Far from being objects that you simply 'flop' into when you're tired, sofas and chairs are the most important pieces of furniture you're likely to choose for the living room—and probably the most expensive overall. Choose with care.

Considerations

A sofa needs to fulfil a variety of needs, including comfort, appearance and versatility, and will be expected to last a lifetime. Which of these you put first depends on your own needs, but it is a mistake to skimp in this area—you should buy the best you can afford.

Ideally, everyone should have their own special chair, built to suit their posture and build. In reality, however, this is impractical and would be vastly expensive.

Testing a chair in a showroom is simply not enough. You have to consider its size, how much support it will give, and whether it will remain comfortable after a few hours.

The sort of comfort given by a chair you automatically sink into like a sack of potatoes is fine in the short term, but will lead to discomfort and backache later on.

Any chair that is going to be used for any length of time should support certain vulnerable parts of the body—namely the back, shoulders and neck—to prevent strain. A chair should also allow for comfort whatever your position in it.

Size could be a major consideration. Many sofas come in both two-seater and three-seater versions, so if only one is on

display, ask whether an alternative can be purchased, possibly to order.

If you're buying a new sofa, or armchair to fit in with existing furniture, consider the relationship between the old and new pieces. As well as design and colour, think about the height and width. For instance, those seated in a chair at a much lower level to others may feel inferior!

Three-piece suites are still a practical and flexible way of arranging furniture layout, but not by any means the only practical choice. You may have rooms that would look better with two two-seater sofas (or even larger), facing each other, with a couple of additional armchairs to supplement the seating.

Fabrics and trim

Don't be put off by display upholstery, either. If you love the shape of a sofa but not its covering, there will most likely be a choice of other fabrics. Manufacturers have vast ranges of colours and patterns, and sample books will be somewhere at hand, if you ask.

Sometimes there is a choice as to whether you'd like decorative features such as piping. This is an ideal way of incorporating colours from your scheme into your furniture without heavy patterns. If you pick a piped sofa or chair, you can then make extra cushions to match, using alternate colours—for example, green scatter cushions with pink piping, to complement a pink sofa that has green piping.

Don't despair if you already have sofas and chairs covered in fabrics that are nothing like the scheme you would ideally like. Most styles can be re-covered —you might even be able to do it yourself. Obviously, though, some designs will be easier to re-cover than others.

As a temporary measure, you can 'cover' up a chair or sofa with rugs—soft

Right: As supplementary seating which is both flexible and portable, floor cushions are hard to beat. Choose covers which co-ordinate with other furnishing fabrics so they blend in with the décor.

dhurries are ideal for this—and indeed this is one means of 'adapting' a room to appear more cozy in winter. Equally, for a summery effect, you could use a pretty lacy bedspread.

Consider fabric qualities when looking at designs, and buy the best you can afford. This may make all the difference to the practical qualities of the sofa or armchair.

Cost is a reasonable guide to quality. Good fabrics do not wear thin, fade, stain, stretch or tear easily. Printed cotton and linen will have a tendency to fade in strong sunlight, and fabrics with a lot of flax tend to wear thin. Although expensive, wool resists dirt naturally, whereas cotton collects it. Man-made fabrics are good, but some have an unattractive surface, whereas mixtures of wool and synthetic fibres combine hardiness with quality.

Always check whether upholstered sofas or chairs are covered with a flame-retardant material; this cannot be judged on price and quality.

Furnishing fabrics are made from fibre in one of three forms—animal, natural or synthetic. Animal fibres include wool and silk; natural include cotton, linen, hemp, jute and ramie; and synthetic fibres consist of viscose, rayon, acetate, nylon, polyester (Terylene, Tergal, Dacron) and acrylic (Orlon, Dralon, Courtelle).

Basically, there are three weaving patterns which make up the finished product—plain, twill and satin, plus numerous variations from these such as Jacquard loom weave which allows for intricate designs. After they are woven, most fabrics are put through finishing processes to help them resist creases, fire, stains and water.

If you're re-covering a chair or sofa yourself, choose plain or small-patterned fabrics. Large-patterned fabric has to be

cut out so that the designs are centred; not only is this more difficult, but it will also lead to more wastage of fabric, which adds to the expense.

Construction materials

As well as upholstery fabric, what the chair is actually constructed from will determine how much it costs, how comfortable it is and its life span.

The frame may be made of wood, metal or plastic. A wooden frame will be of either a quality wood or ramin offcuts —the price will reflect the difference. The advantage of a wooden frame is that re-upholstery is a fairly uncomplicated process.

Metal frames are usually made up of steel tubes with webbing attached to support the seat and back. Fully upholstered seating rarely has metal frames, but semi-upholstered may. Watch out for fixings—badly joined metal might become a weak spot.

The advantage of plastic frames is that they are very light, but the consistency of the material means that damage to the frame is irreparable.

All-foam seating usually comes in the form of flexible sofa beds, but has never really taken off as an alternative to permanent timber, metal or plastic seating.

Seating pads are generally made of foam. The advantage of this up to now is that it has always been cheap and is easy to manufacture. Its main disadvantage is that it is highly inflammable, since it's made from petro-chemicals. The alternatives are horse hair, feathers and other such materials. These tend to be expensive, but they are beginning to be manufactured more than foam because of its inflammability and the rising prices of oil.

Other forms of seating

Flexibility is the secret of any seating arrangement. It will have to cater not only for any family get-togethers (as a

Left: Built-in seating with comfortable cushions is easy to construct and makes good use of the available space. A cupboard underneath would be easy to include as well, stretching the space even further.

Right: Cool, clean colours combine with ultra-modern furnishings to create a futuristic dining room. The harmonizing colour of the table increases the light, airy, spacious feeling.

comfortable area to view television, to talk, to keep warm, and so on), but also for times when there are more people than normal (visiting grannies, friends, neighbours). For additional seating you can choose between permanent and temporary types. Permanent additional seating may take the form of a reclining chair, a rocker, a chaise-longue or a leather stool, for example.

Garden chairs made of bamboo or cane can be made full use of during the winter if they're brought indoors and 'warmed up' with squashy cushions for the seat and back, or draped with fabric.

You can also smarten up old wooden kitchen chairs, for example bentwood chairs, by rubbing them down and painting them in a colour that matches your scheme. Then either leave them plain, or add a seat cushion. An extra touch is to paint a design on the seat and/or back, freehand or using stencils. Originally meant for more practical use in the kitchen, they'll look great in the living room—all you need is a little imagination.

Good furniture stores have ranges of furniture that fall into the category of permanent seating, in the form of occasional chairs. Most are in stunning modern designs and might be considered a luxury.

Temporary seating is a boon if you've budgeted for a sofa yet need extra seating without being able to afford matching chairs. Folding chairs are available in a myriad of designs, prices and colours, so you should have little trouble finding them to suit your scheme or your pocket.

They come in a variety of materials like perspex, canvas, wood and metal. The advantage of these is that if they become surplus to your requirements at any time, you can simply unfold them and store them away in a cupboard. Hang them on hooks and they are completely

out of the way, even if storage space is short and they're hung on the living room wall!

Whether you need them normally or not, folding chairs are a valuable addition to any home. They mean that extra seating can be obtained immediately at times like Christmas when visitors seem never-ending.

Dining chairs often perform a variety of purposes besides seating for meals. If you are choosing chairs to go with a table already in your possession, make sure they are the right height to give sufficient leg room—measure before you shop around. If the chairs have arms, ensure that they will fit under the table easily; this is important if they have to be pushed out of the way to save space.

Dining chairs must be comfortable to sit in and easily pushed away from the table when the meal is over. If you choose flexible folding chairs here, you can keep just a couple out permanently and store the remainder away until needed.

If dining chairs are required as occasional seating as well as for dining, ensure they will look as comfortable in the living room area as around the dining table.

All kinds of tables

There are tables for dining, for coffee cups, for games, for lighting—the list is endless. Put these all together and you'll probably envisage exactly what most people have . . . far too many tables.

Ideally, tables should be practical first and stylish second—or at least an equal balance of the two. Of course, having lots of tables is fine if you also have masses of space. But if space is short, it's probably better having one unit to take on the many roles performed by different tables.

If necessary, a dining table can take on a variety of functions, just like dining chairs—in fact, it may become the most

useful table you have. Designs, materials, shapes, sizes and prices of tables vary so considerably that the uninitiated may feel overwhelmed at first.

Don't make up your mind straight away. Once you've decided on what sort of table you need for a certain room or function, look around to see how certain shapes and designs look in different settings. Department stores usually

arrange their furniture in suitable settings and in window displays. You could also look at wallpaper books, especially if you've already picked a design, to see what sort of furniture they have chosen.

Finishes come in a variety of materials such as perspex, glass, metal, plastic, marble, paint, formica; there's something to suit everyone.

Dining tables
Every home needs a civilized place to serve food, and a dining table of some sort is the only efficient way to do this. This applies to three-course dinner parties as much as help-yourself buffets. Estimate how many people will, on average, fit around the table. Each diner should feel comfortable and not be jogging someone else in the elbow every time they lift a

fork to their mouth. On average a table that can seat six comfortably will satisfy most needs. You may want to buy one that extends to seat, say, eight for special occasions. Remember, a round table will take up less space than a rectangular one.

Of course if space is extremely limited, a table to seat four will have to suffice and will usually be flexible enough to take six at a squeeze. Guests will understand

Above: A dining room in the traditional style relies upon beautifully finished wood like mahogany, together with velvet, brocade or damask upholstery. Silver, crystal and bone china are also important ingredients.

81

Below right: Free-standing storage units like this blend well with either modern or traditional furnishings and will display ornaments to great advantage, as well as holding stereo equipment, drinks, glasses, books and any other items you need in the living room.

these space problems, especially if it's a first-time buy or a young person's flat. Sometimes a casual buffet supper is more practical for serving where space is limited.

Typing, writing, sewing, dining may all cause damage to table surfaces, especially those made of wood, so some sort of protection is needed. A tablecloth alone will not do—make sure you have mats or some form of protection that can be slipped under the top layer of cloth.

Scale should be kept in mind when considering all furniture, and tables are no exception. The relationship between the table and its surroundings—either other furniture or the room scheme—is important. A glass-topped table, for example, will not only allow more light into an area but will make the table look smaller than it is. A heavy oak table will have the opposite effect.

If a dining table expands (by flaps or by having a split top), keep it at its smallest except when the expansion is needed. This will make maximum use of floor space and will be quite adequate for other purposes, like studying. If your dining table is in the living room, it can be pushed against the wall out of the way. When not in use, it can be used as a display area, with a simply arranged vase of flowers and a picture or two on the adjacent wall above. Chairs can either be stored away or used practically in other rooms (the hall, for example).

Occasional tables

Coffee tables are either loved or hated—there's no in-between. Sometimes they become useless items that simply attract clutter and become an excuse for not putting things away. If space is really at a premium, it is probably better to dispense altogether with a coffee table and have one or two small sofa tables by the side of chairs on which to put cups, magazines, ashtrays, etc.

When space is of no consequence, there are some very stylish low tables that look superb in a large setting.

The size of occasional tables must relate to the height of the chairs you have. Before buying, measure what you would consider comfortable for reaching the table. Bear in mind that small tables to go at the ends of sofas should ideally be about the same height as the sides of the sofa, or just a little below, so you will not have to reach over the arms to use the tables.

Coffee table height is important too. People must be able to see each other across the table, without moving, what-ever things have been placed on top of it.

Most good furniture manufacturers make ranges that include matching coffee and side tables (as well as storage units), if you want uniformity.

Hall tables need to be higher than those in the living room, usually to take the telephone and perhaps directories stored beneath. If the telephone is in the living room, however, you will probably want to answer it from the comfort of your armchair, so that table should be as high as required.

Clever storage

Everybody needs some sort of storage, but how much depends on habits, person-ality and tastes. If you're the sort of person who throws everything away that's useless or valueless, you'll need less than the type who hoards all kinds of paraphernalia.

Don't be restricted as to *where* you store things—if the only available space for extra bookshelves is in the hall or bed-room, put them there. Bookshelves will make *any* room look cozy and homely.

Living room storage

If your household is a family home, this will be the most universally shared room. As such, there must be a certain amount

Above: Room dividers provide a visual break in long through rooms and can help to increase storage space too.

of storage to contain generally used items, especially if there isn't a separate dining room. Built-in wall units are the neatest and most convenient way to store things in a living room and still retain floor space.

If arranged properly, built-in units can take the place of most other items of furniture. One unit along a wall can hold tv, stereo, video, records, speakers, cassettes, cutlery, games, books, glasses, bottles and stationery (and more!), all at once, yet taking up limited floor space. This leaves the rest of the room free for living and feeling comfortable in. It really depends on what you want to hide away, and what you prefer to be left on show.

A wall unit can be as low or high as you want and can even act as a room divider. Some are accessible from both sides so that a cut-off dining area has an easily accessible place to store all dining necessities, separate from living room clutter. Some may even incorporate a pull-down bureau, useful if there is nowhere to write letters or study. Choice is purely a matter of taste—there are styles to suit everyone, from reproduction Tudor oak ranges to pure-looking Scandinavian yew.

Freestanding storage units come in all sorts of materials and designs. Very popular is the type usually made with a metal frame, with shelving in wood, glass, formica-covered chipboard or metal. These units can be bought one by one if the budget is tight, eventually to build up a whole wall.

As long as the shelving is adjustable, these are as versatile as built-in storage. Some are made to take drawers and cupboards from the same range, added and bought as individual elements.

If you plan to use such 'solid' storage, make sure you have enough power points on the wall behind to take all the electrical goods. Remember that hi-fi's

and televisions need a certain amount of ventilation to function correctly—if in doubt, call in a specialist for advice. Speakers should ideally not be too close together or you may spoil the stereo effect—a great shame if you've bought a particularly good system.

If you have acquired, or prefer, separate pieces of living room storage, make full use of them. Old Victorian wardrobes, for example, too big for the bedroom, make wonderful living room cupboards and you can add extra shelves if need be. Old washstands with marble tops need not be restricted to the bedroom or kitchen. They also make a delightful centrepiece in the living or dining room, and the perfect medium on which to display collections of ornaments or pictures.

The key to successful storage is to use it well and, to a certain extent, keep it tidy. It will probably be one of the focal points in a room, so books should not be stacked haphazardly, or paraphernalia simply thrown on to the shelves.

If you're keeping lots of items with different functions on the shelving, using additional containers will make it neater. Wire office trays or baskets, for example, will keep stationery needs, small toys and pens tidy and at hand. Records should be stored upright to keep them in good condition and easily accessible, and cassettes arranged in book-like rows.

Select a certain wall or space for storage and use it to the full. By expanding upwards and sideways you'll have a block of well arranged storage that's not only efficient in practice, but looks good as well.

Dining room storage

A separate dining room may be needed for many other purposes besides dining. It might double as a guest room, a study, a sewing room or a playroom, and the

type and amount of storage furniture will depend on these uses, as well as the size of the room.

It is better to have all table setting items—cutlery, glasses, napkins, even china—near at hand, so that the person preparing the table will not be a continual interruption to those in the kitchen.

If there is enough room, valuable china can also be stored safely in the dining

surface, either make sure it will withstand heat or add mats to protect it.

Bedroom furniture

Don't put a bed at the bottom of your priority list. We spend a vast portion of our lives asleep, and an unsuitable bed that seems only a bit uncomfortable at first can lead to a variety of physical complaints later on.

It's best never to buy secondhand; a bed that has been worn into a certain shape by one person can give another all sorts of problems.

Also, never replace a mattress without buying a new divan as well; otherwise, the new mattress will simply develop the same faults as the previous one.

Choosing a bed

It is recommended that an adult have a new bed every ten years—and you should spend every penny you can afford on the best, each time you buy.

Left: Home-made living room shelving like this is practical as well as bright and stylish. It can be extended to make it longer or higher or to fit round a corner or out into the room as a divider. Above: The free-standing cube is an extremely versatile storage unit all around the house. Apart from combining well with other cubes to form novel shapes, it is attractive and simple.

room—leaving less valuable pieces in the kitchen for more informal meals.

A traditional dresser is ideal for the dining room, providing space for china, glasses, bottles, cutlery and table linen, as well as a serving area. Glass-fronted designs also keep china free from dust and dirt and prevent splashes whilst food is being served. Look around secondhand shops and manufacturers who make natural wood furniture, but be prepared to pay a lot for an item such as this. Modern versions, however, tend to be quite deep, so measure how big the maximum depth can be before you buy.

Some living room furniture is ideal for use in the dining room. A sideboard or serving top can be incorporated within a run of such wall units.

If you're putting hot dishes on to any

Right and far right: Light bedding fabrics contrast dramatically with rich, dark wood and ornate carving to create beds with a truly romantic feeling.

If you're really short of space, opt for a bed with some sort of integral storage facility, such as those with drawers at the base.

There are a few general rules to follow when buying. The heavier you are, the firmer the bed should be. Consider the length too: a bed should be at least 17cm longer than you. A very tall person may need to spend more on a custom-made bed to ensure it is long enough for comfort.

Partners who share a bed may not necessarily find an all-in-one double the ideal choice. If one person is heavier than the other, or one prefers a firmer bed, separate mattresses that 'zip' together may be better. Some twin beds can be clipped together.

Look around and give yourself plenty of time to choose—and, however embarrassing, you should always test the bed to see how comfortable it is. Sitting on it won't suffice—you should really lie on it for a true test, and with your partner, if you are looking for a bed for both of you.

Mattresses

The mattress should provide support for your entire body. Check for complete comfort by moving around in different sleep positions. Always make sure a bed is wide enough, and stretch out full-length as well. Never be swayed by the fabric pattern that the mattress is covered with—it won't show once the bed is made-up. It's the internal quality that counts.

There are three basic forms of mattress —solid foam, stuffed and interior sprung. A good foam mattress should be at least 11cm thick, otherwise it is not worth buying.

The amount of support in stuffed mattresses depends on the resilience and the quality of the filling, plus whether or not there is a sprung base as support. There are two types of sprung mattress interior—pocket springs and open springs. The denser the springs, the better.

Pocket springs are individually contained so that each spring is unaffected by compression from others. This is ideal for double beds.

Open spring mattresses are made up of a network of springs.

The average amount of springs in both types of mattress is 500, with a recommended minimum of 288. Some have up to 1,000. Price will be a good indicator of this—the higher the number of springs, the higher the price and the better quality the bed. If you're not sure about quantities of springs, check with the retailer.

Divans

Bed bases are usually sprung-edged or firm-edged. Sprung-edge divans are the most expensive, but are formed in such a way that they help prolong the life of the mattress. Firm-edge divans are cheaper and higher off the ground than sprung-edge bases.

Bed frames

The type of frame is a matter of choice, depending quite often on what style is required, how much you want to spend, and how large you want it to be.

Since the bedroom is the place where personal preference can be given most consideration, you can really go to town.

Iron frames are wonderful to look at and very sturdy, but they tend to be extremely heavy. If you want a sense of the past, a four-poster might be right, but it should only be considered for a room that can take the scale—they do look rather silly squeezed into a small space. You can create a four-poster effect by fixing lightweight curtain poles from the ceiling; lengths of sheer fabric or lace can then be hung from pole rings.

Alternative beds

For guests, you can get by with cheaper beds, as they won't be used regularly by one person. Divan beds that can be made into a sofa during the day are also ideal for guest rooms.

If you fancy Japanese-style living, or prefer not having a bed base at all, a futon may be the answer. Originally, futons

were temporary sleeping mattresses that could be rolled up during the day. European versions tend to be fairly heavy, however, so this sort of quick removal can be difficult. They are made of cotton, stuffed with cotton wadding, and provide solid support as well as comfort.

So-called orthopedic beds have nothing to do with medical recommendations— the use of the word is purely related to the hardness of the mattress.

Folding beds tend to be nothing more than camp beds, so aren't suitable for permanent sleeping. However, they're very useful as emergency stand-bys— especially if you've lots of teenage visitors, who'll treat the idea of sleeping on one as fun and adventurous.

Waterbeds are becoming more popular, but they are extremely heavy, containing about 150 gallons of water, so the floor must be able to take the weight. This is probably unlikely in small, modern houses, so it's best to get advice on this before you buy one. Waterbeds are extremely expensive, still being in the luxury end of the market.

Sleeping modules are the futuristic side of bedroom furniture. They are usually astronomical in price and often make strong use of shiny, gilt, marbled or velvety materials. Such modules usually combine a king-size bed (often in an unconventional shape), dimmable lighting system, stereo cassette/radio, alarm and so on. All a bit too much in price, size and design for the average person—they tend to be more fun to look at than anything!

Headboards

Headboards are a matter of choice, and a wide range of styles makes this easy. If, however, you find a wooden or metal headboard too hard-looking, you can make your own from quilted fabric— perhaps in a pattern matching the bed

Far left: Curtains hanging from poles suspended from ceiling joists make a light, airy but still cozy and private sleeping area. Left above: Pretty pastel colours and a 'storybook' duvet are well suited to a little girl's room. Left below: Some styles of headboard can be covered in the same fabric as bed linen and other furnishings, for a fully co-ordinated look.

linen—and hang it from a short curtain pole at the head of the bed.

Having chosen a bed with as much care as possible, you'll want to decide what other furniture you'll need in a bedroom. There are countless styles of furniture especially for this purpose, so first think of the practical considerations.

Wardrobes and cupboards

Everyone needs some sort of storage to

Far left: Bright, cheery wallpaper and co-ordinating bed linen, cushions, tablecloth and lampshade make a delightful room for a young girl. Centre left: With the help of well-chosen cushions and a long bed canopy hanging elegantly over the bedhead, this bedroom has a smart, comfortable style set off by just a few accessories. The two types of carpet also accentuate the bed area. Left: A four-poster bed adds a touch of elegance to any bedroom but can be expensive. This bed uses ordinary curtain rails suspended from ceiling joists to achieve a similar effect at much lower cost.

keep clothes in, including hanging space. Obviously a wardrobe is the ideal item to start with.

A walk-in, wall-to-wall wardrobe may seem like the most practical and glamorous solution, but will be a waste if by having it you're simply cutting the bedroom down to a ridiculous size.

Some bedrooms already have built-in cupboards. Consider adding a mirror front—this will not only provide you with a useful, full-length mirror but will reflect light and make the room look bigger.

The best way to utilize space in any cupboard is to arrange the inside carefully —and often. Otherwise, valuable space is just wasted. If the rail is fixed too high, for example, the space at the bottom may not be used enough. By adding a shelf at the bottom, you'll use the redundant space and provide a section specially for

shoes, away from other items. If the cupboard or wardrobe itself is very high, and the rail is fixed fairly low down, the alternative would be to add a shelf at the top, or even another hanging rail for shorter items like shirts or skirts.

If there appears to be no space to put cupboards, re-think the room. They can be built in anywhere, not just in an alcove or along a wall. Make use of what would otherwise seem a wasted wall by building

them around a window. Alternatively, erect them on the wall next to the door. If you include a cupboard *above* the door, you will have made a deep entrance that will frame the door and act as a passage within the room.

Other storage alternatives

If money does not run to built-in or free-standing wardrobes of any kind, you can fix a rail along one wall and disguise it with a run of curtains, blinds or louvre doors (painted to match the décor). Fabrics make a very versatile covering of this kind; you are not restricted as to what you use, since it can easily be removed for cleaning and can be pulled open without taking up room space. Choice really depends on the style of room and decoration colours.

Louvre doors are very good value and look professional. If you're really adventurous, individual louvres can be painted in different colours, to match your scheme, and fixed in whatever combination you want. Louvres that fold concertina fashion when open will take up minimum space.

Wire and cane baskets are useful for keeping underclothes, socks and shoes in one place, but tights and stockings should not be kept in cane baskets as they are likely to snag.

Keep baskets out of the way by mounting them on the wall; use hooks or rings so they can be removed at will.

Most people need somewhere next to the bed for lamps, books or a cup and saucer. This need not be the conventional type of bedside table, although there are lots of acceptable ranges of bedroom furniture which incorporate them.

Any type of small table will do, and even if you're having to make do with something you consider quite ugly, you can cover up a multitude of sins using floor-length cloths to match the scheme.

Right: This storage chest has been painted and trimmed with a border to co-ordinate with the wallpaper so it blends unobtrusively into the room.

Left: A self-assembly wardrobe along the length of a wall makes an efficient storage area in a bedroom. Above: Storage cubes follow the roof slope in this children's playroom, making maximum use of space which would otherwise be wasted.

Chests of drawers and dressing tables
A certain amount of furniture, apart from the wardrobe, may be needed for storing clothing.

Chests of drawers are still popular and, as with most bedroom furniture, there's great interest in buying up old pieces, usually pine, then stripping and restoring them if necessary. Such pieces can still be found quite cheaply. Quite often local auction rooms are good hunting grounds.

Chests can double up as dressing table surfaces if need be, with either a mirror fixed on the wall above or a freestanding model placed on top. Lack of leg room is the only real problem with this.

Dressing tables need plenty of light, so they shouldn't be hidden in corners.

Those with deep drawers are best; some even have special pull-out cosmetic trays. Chairs to go with dressing tables should be at a comfortable height—check this if you're buying them separately.

Small drawer units can be adapted to make a dressing table. Add an extra surface across the top of two units, leaving space in the middle for legs.

Above, right and far right: This studio bed will double as a couch in a teenager's bedroom. It makes the most of the space it occupies by providing storage inside the divan base and in the large trunk at the head of the bed, as well as shelves along the side.

Children's rooms

The basic necessities for children's rooms are hanging and drawer space for clothes, shelf space for books, storage space for toys and work surfaces for homework, hobbies or nursery equipment.

Children's bedrooms need to be flexible, especially if the children are young, as their needs change the older they get. While they do not need large wardrobes and other items of furniture whilst they're small, beware of buying

furniture that will become limited in use in the future because of its size. There are special children's ranges that are not only appealing to children but also practical, and will remain so in years to come, when the children are older.

Beds that incorporate some form of storage are ideal, leaving floor space free. Children should not have bunk beds until they are at least four years old. The best designs are those that can be separated into single beds when the children are older. However, check that they're really stable, have lockable safety catches to prevent accidental parting of the beds and have ladders that are safe. Many may look terrific, especially to children, but may be hazardous.

Teenagers will appreciate a divan bed that can be made into a sofa during the day, when their friends come round.

It is a good idea to have somewhere special to put toys, especially if you consider instilling tidiness important. A large, old chest is perfect, as toys can be thrown in easily. There must also be a variety of surfaces for hobbies, homework or nursery equipment.

Stacking units with drawers, shelves and doors are ideal for incorporating storage space in a child's room, with the bright, modern look they will like.

These usually provide useful surface space (for dolls, models, etc), which is wipe-clean for easy maintenance.

Wooden furniture can be painted in exciting, highly coloured designs, and a redundant easy chair that's of little value will be most useful.

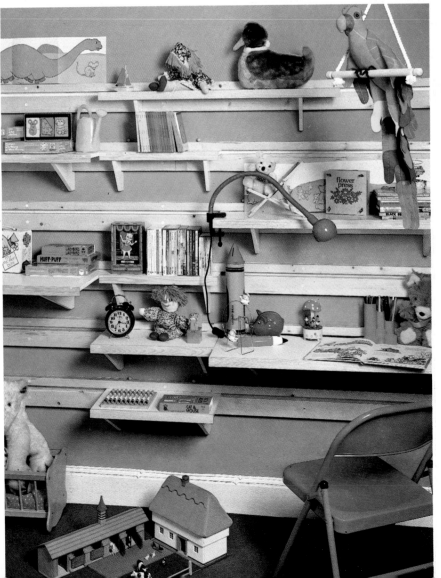

Far left: Wallpaper and bed linen featuring favourite cartoon characters are bound to be popular with young children. Left: A modular shelving system will grow with your child and provides an excellent place to keep toys and books within easy reach.

95

CHAPTER 9

Finishing touches

A beautifully decorated and furnished room always looks so
much nicer with the scattered personal touches and chosen
possessions that make it an individual home.

*I*t is the little things that matter. This doesn't mean collecting a badly thought-out selection of clutter—there is a difference between careful groupings of collectables, and hoards of possessions strewn about in any fashion.

Fireplaces and mantelpieces

Those who have old fireplaces are lucky. Not only are they usually lovely to look at, but they aid ventilation in a room, helping to prevent condensation; don't block them up if you can possibly help it.

Restored and then either left bare or painted to enhance their beauty, they make the perfect place for displays, especially if the mantelpiece is deep.

In winter you'll have one of the most envied of heating systems, an open fire. (But beware of thinking you need no other form of heating—an open fire alone is not sufficient.) When it's not in use, you can make the fireplace into a focal point by using the open grate to display an object of your choice such as a large, beautiful vase filled with masses of fresh or dried flowers. If it's big enough, and

the chimney is blocked up, you can even keep the television there!

Displaying collections

Rooms reflect your personality, not just by the decoration schemes you choose, but also by the things you have in them. It doesn't matter if the knick-knacks you love so much aren't valuable —sentimental value can mean just as much and may be less easily replaced. However, if you own or collect valuable pieces, you'll want to display them in the best way possible.

Left: The individually styled fireplace in this bedroom uses a panel of patterned tiles in both sides of the surround, blending perfectly with the wall covering and feminine feel of the bedroom. Below: Pelargoniums, primulas and African violets provide a scented, flowery cover for a summer fireplace.

Below and right: Collections do not have to be large and expensive to be attractive. Cotton reels and scissors (near right) hung from nails on a board, and rings on dummy hands make a most effective display. French bon bon tins (far right, above) can be secured to a simple framework. Silver spoons (far right, below) in a variety of shapes and sizes hung from a wooden display rack make an elegant wall decoration. Even toys (below) can make interesting articles for display.

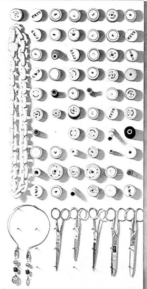

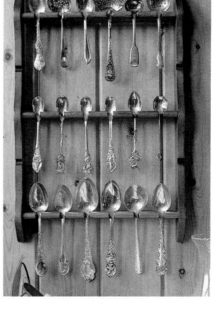

It is a rare bird who collects nothing. The modern interpretation seems to be that anything is collectable—from glass bottles to match books, from old utensils to miniature soaps—and the best way to enjoy them is to somehow display them. Keeping a collection haphazardly in a box, to be brought out once a year, seems a shame when it could make a colourful addition to a room.

Bottles are a favourite. They look best displayed in a spot where the light can shine through them—by a window, for example.

Special china or porcelain is often arranged inside display cabinets with glass doors. This keeps it free from dust and reduces the chances of its being broken, especially if there are young children or animals in the house. A light inside the cabinet will show the china off fully.

Corner cabinets take up little space. Modern ones are available in a wide variety of styles and materials, although you can still find antique and old ones, usually at a price.

Consider what you are displaying and the type of room scheme the cabinet is going into. A reproduction Georgian cabinet, for example, would look totally out of place in a very modern setting, whereas a collection of toby jugs might look equally odd displayed in a sleek 20th century Swedish cabinet made of yew. Decide on a happy medium for both the cabinet and the ornaments, then you'll satisfy all needs. The only problem with special display cabinets is that quite often there are bars holding glass in place which may obscure the display slightly.

Collections do not have to be specialized and costly to look good—anything from old cotton reels, sets of finely shaped keys or modern tins will be desirable and interesting if they're displayed well.

Shelves are good for showing off anything, although items on exposed ones will get more dusty than in a cabinet with glass doors to protect them.

If you don't mind the extra work they might incur, shelving systems are excellent for displaying anything, especially larger items like old cameras and foreign dolls. Their main advantage over closed cabinets is that you can see everything very clearly. And with open shelving items can be seen from both sides, which might be preferable for some collections.

Printers' trays (originally used for keeping printing blocks in place) are good for displaying tiny objects like thimbles and shells—if you can find one, that is. However much bargaining you might have to do, they're worth having, as they are becoming more and more scarce these days. They can be hung on the wall quite easily.

Make sure that anything you fix on the

wall to display your possessions is very securely fastened to avoid disasters and distress!

Larger items, for example old blanket chests, milk urns, small round tables of real or sentimental value or even stunning modern pieces of furniture, are collectable in themselves. While they remain practical for holding or displaying things, they also have the distinction of being items to look at for their own merit.

Choosing pictures

Pictures are the most popular way of decorating the walls of a home, adding colour and interest. If chosen appropriately, they can also emphasize and reinforce your style of decoration.

Personal taste is the most important priority when choosing pictures. Never pick one simply because you think it's the right thing to do—choose it only because you genuinely like the picture

Left: A noticeboard made of garden trellis provides an interesting and attractive place to put all those odd bits and pieces no one likes to throw away.
Above: A country look has been given to a plain wall by displaying decorative dried grasses and colourful flower pictures around a serving hatch.

Straight line

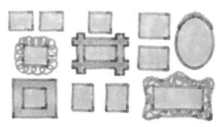

Rectangular block

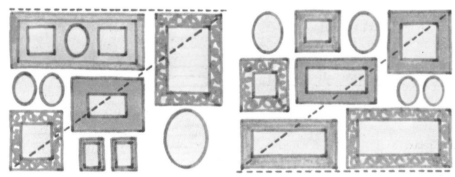

Diagonal line

Classic proportions

Circle

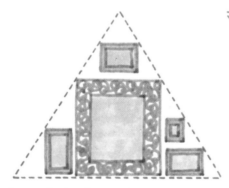

Inverted triangle

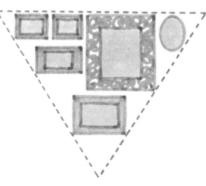

Triangle

Above: Groupings of pictures look best if they follow a particular shape, such as those illustrated here.

pictures. It helps to think of the entire group as a particular shape. For instance, you can arrange them in a straight line, placing the largest picture in the centre for balance. Alternatively, they could go in a square or rectangular block, which is particularly effective when the pictures are the same size. For pictures of different sizes and shapes, you could arrange the block round a diagonal line, as though it were two triangles.

For classic proportions, position two small pictures, one above the other, alongside a larger picture, so that the height-to-width proportion of the rectangle they form is three-to-five.

A circular grouping, with or without a picture in the centre, is a good way to display round or oval frames. And a triangle is an alternative to the diagonal line for displaying pictures of different sizes and shapes.

Be sure to take into account the amount of wall space and also the size of nearby furniture when planning the extent of the grouping. If you want to make your ceiling look higher, a vertical arrangement will help. Equally, to lower a too high ceiling, try a horizontal grouping.

Plain walls will make all pictures stand out better than patterned walls. On patterns you'll need a thicker frame or mount, whereas on a plain wall a simple band of colour, wood or metal might be sufficient.

What to look for

Galleries and art shops these days offer a good selection of frames as well as prints in a choice of materials (woods and metals), colours and thicknesses.

Oil paintings are still popular, but don't rely on one gaining greatly in value just because of the medium that has been used to paint it. There is always the chance that it might, of course, especially

(unless, of course, you are a specialist).

Nowadays, art is accessible to everyone. You don't have to spend a fortune to buy nice prints; good frames are now readily available at reasonable prices.

Always consider the size of a room when choosing pictures. A picture should look in proportion to a wall; it should neither swamp a small wall, nor

look like a postage stamp on a generous-sized one. If you can't get the right size of print for a certain wall, then arrange several little ones in a group. Avoid leaving one picture looking lonely on a vast blank space.

Group displays

Put some thought into the grouping of

if it is by a new artist who later gains in popularity. But unless you are an expert, you'd be better off buying something because you like it rather than because of high hopes for its future value.

You don't have to be a millionaire to own oil paintings. They can still be found in secondhand shops and antique markets; quite often seaside towns are good hunting grounds. And who knows? You may well be the one-in-a-thousand accidental owner of a future Van Gogh.

Watercolours have a charm all of their own because of the translucent nature of the medium used. They tend to be cheaper than oils because they take less time to execute and the paint is cheaper.

As for reproductions, the quality depends on the paper and printing, so look very closely. Good reproductions will be very close to the original in colour. Some copies of famous oil paintings are treated to look like canvas.

Original prints range considerably in price, so there's something to suit every pocket. Sometimes they come in sets, so you can co-ordinate easily with three or four prints. Don't be tempted by offers of limited editions that will increase in value, unless you know a great deal about the art market.

Photographs make charming displays of family history, especially if you have any well preserved photographs of distant relations. Alternatively, Victorian, Edwardian or other early photographs which you can pick up in antique and secondhand shops make fascinating viewing. Those taken by pioneer photographers or depicting famous ladies of the past tend to be rather more expensive than anonymous versions.

Posters are very colourful, and are likely to find their way on to the walls of growing teenagers. Cheap and cheerful, they will brighten up a dull spare room or pander to the whims of a besotted

16-year-old. More desirable for general display are those that depict old soap or cosmetic advertisements, of, say, the 1920s (great for bathrooms), or reproduction wartime posters which may bring a touch of nostalgia.

Anything can be framed—old birthday cards, music sheets, diplomas, children's drawings—and used most effectively as decoration.

The type of light that pictures are illuminated with may make a difference to the effect the viewer receives from them. Avoid strong direct sunlight; some papers may turn yellow, or the printing inks go blue. If you want to highlight a particular picture, special picture lights are ideal, forcing a beam to shine directly on to the subject. This may be more advantageous to oil or watercolour paintings than any other.

As an alternative to pictures, you could consider covering a pinboard with interesting postcards, snapshots from family get-togethers, menus, invitations, theatre tickets and so on to brighten up a kitchen or hall. Whatever's pinned there, everyone will want to stop to look.

Bedrooms and spare rooms

Personality really can come to the fore in your bedroom. (And the same applies to children's bedrooms, if they're allowed a certain amount of licence there.) Once you've chosen which style the room is to be decorated in and decided on furniture, you can add the little bits and pieces that make it into the type of room you've always wanted and in which you can really relax.

Little touches like cushions, tie-backs, pictures and perfume bottles personalize

Left: There are many delightful bits and pieces you can add to a bedroom to make it reflect your personality and tastes.

Right: Pretty Victorian-style fringed lampshades in fabrics that co-ordinate with your furnishings are easy to make and cast a soft glow over ornaments displayed nearby. Far right: Trimming curtains and wallpaper with multi-coloured satin ribbon is a pretty way to brighten up a child's room.

a bedroom and give it texture and interest at the same time.

Bedlinen can make or break a bedroom. These days, however, there is such a great selection of patterns and colours that choosing it is easier than ever.

Designs can often be bought to co-ordinate with wallpaper ranges. This does away with the headache of having to choose yet another pattern or design to complete a room—especially appealing if you've already exhausted your imagination elsewhere! Don't, however, take the easy way out just for the sake of it. Different patterns can blend together very well (see page 12).

Of course, you don't have to have pattern on the bed at all; a plain cover may look just as inviting. If you want to add interest, simply throw a few cushions on to the bed, possibly made from fabrics that co-ordinate with wallpaper, curtains or other designs in the room. Cushions are very easy to make for any room and with a little patience you can produce some which are at least as good quality as anything you'd buy.

Lamps are nice in a bedroom, giving a soft, romantic glow. For reading in bed, however, you'll need something stronger to see by, such as a spotlight or special reading lamp. There are lots of styles and colours around and you're bound to find one that suits you.

If you want to hide ugly bed legs, team a valance with your bedcover. It will not only be practical, but will add a soft look to the bed.

You can make your own pillowcases in a style to suit you, if you don't like the choice available. You can add borders, a frill, lace or embroidery, or simply use a fabric of your choice to make them into odd shapes or larger sizes than usual.

If you can't find a lampshade style that you like, then simply make your own. You can use fabrics that ready-made ones

might not come in, or make other designs like pleated or handkerchief-style shades, for a softer look.

Bolsters can provide a nice finishing touch to a bed. They finish off the style, making it crisp and clean-looking, and can also be used as efficient armrests. They hide the top of the bed nicely too.

Soften the walls by hanging rugs that seem too good to walk on. If you choose colours to match the scheme, they'll co-ordinate nicely as well as giving a cozy atmosphere to the room.

Flowers and plants don't have to be restricted to 'public' rooms like the living room—they'll look just as lovely in the bedroom or spare room.

If the main bedroom's big enough, an old sofa will add a luxurious touch, especially if you pile it high with cushions. It can be turned into a practical chaise longue—comfortable for when you need a quiet sit-down away from the rest of the household. It may also turn an empty corner into an attractive focal point.

If plumbing's no problem, an extra basin in the bedroom will be most useful. Even better, add an en-suite bathroom (or just a shower). Among other conveniences, this saves fighting for the main bathroom in the morning.

Children's rooms

Kids' rooms will probably evolve into their areas with personal additions of their choice. The age of the child will make a difference—the older they are, the more 'precious' they'll be about arranging their territory the way they want it. You'll probably have more chance of putting your hand to work in their rooms when they're younger.

Scraps of old fabric can be used to make a wonderful, picturesque patchwork wall-hanging for a child's room. If the colours are varied and bright, young ones will be

fascinated. Mobiles are easy to make, too.

Crates and storage boxes of any kind are especially useful for toys. They're handy in the spare room as well.

Baskets, wickerwork and cane look good anywhere, including the bedroom. If it's old or dull, just spray it in a toning colour. Badly damaged cane or wicker should be taken to an expert for repair. Baskets can be used to hold a variety of objects, from make-up to collections of painted eggs.

Old hats hung on the wall will have special memories, especially if they're left over from school days.

Living and dining rooms

Living areas don't have to be impersonal just because they're 'on show'. There is plenty of scope for making living and dining rooms reflect your own individuality.

Lamps are particularly important here. Never pick models that are too small, or they'll look stingy. Be bold and have a look at a slightly larger size than you'd initially thought of. Sometimes, the larger the lamp, the more impressive it is.

Plants can really come into their own in living and dining rooms. Groupings of potted palms look great and add a vibrant, luscious look. Pot holders don't have to cost a lot; plain white ones look perfectly adequate, especially if you've healthy plants that hide most of the bases anyway. You can treat yourself to more luxurious ones when money allows. The most unlikely items can be used to hold plants—for example, a large teapot with a broken lid will become useful and decorative again when cuttings are planted in it.

Big, beautiful books are worth buying for coffee table reading. They're quite a worthwhile investment, as hours of pleasure can be obtained from them. Buy only those you are genuinely interested in, as

hardbacks are usually fairly expensive.

Musical instruments look good on display, especially if they're old. If you have a piano, look after it; if it's an old one it may still have its original candle holders, which will look lovely in their intended use.

Any bare brick in the living or dining room shouldn't be wasted. Hang pictures, brasses, portraits on the wall—the beauty of the brick will only be enhanced by interesting additions, and it will show through to great advantage.

A round or square corner table will be the ideal place to gather a collection of free-standing family portraits. Collections of such frames look good together, even if they're different in style, and are ideally placed in the living room where visitors gather.

Radiators need not stay the colour they arrived in. Either paint them to match the scheme or, if they're particularly ugly, hide them behind trellis or special radiator grilles. (Do expect to lose some heat, however, when you cover a radiator in this way.)

Appropriately coloured pot-pourri will enhance a pretty bowl and will be lastingly decorative. (This is not advisable with young children around, however, as they're likely to eat it!) Table-top displays might be best kept on pretty trays—not only to keep them nicely arranged but so that they can be easily removed for furniture to be cleaned.

Conjure up the epicurean atmosphere in a dining area by hanging collections of old plates on the walls.

Excess kitchen 'things' such as copper pans, old pots, china of any sort, can all look good in the dining area. Such items are usually interesting in shape, so it seems a shame not to display them in one way or another.

Table linen is best kept close at hand in a drawer or cupboard. Keep matching

napkins and cloths together so you don't have to hunt around for the odd napkin when you need them. It's best to have more than one set of linen in case unexpected guests happen to arrive while one set is in the wash.

Left and above: Houseplants bring life and colour into the home. They can be used singly or in groups, in a wide variety of containers or even on a classic marblized plinth like the one shown here.

CHAPTER 10

Living in style

It's not difficult to adapt traditional ideas to suit modern
living without sacrificing style. The look of your home can
reflect any mood or period you like.

o you have definite ideas about how you want your furnished rooms to look? If you have a style in mind, carry on—you'll need no further help and it's what suits you that's best. If, on the other hand, you like several things and can't quite decide on a specific style, you may wonder what to look for.

Finding a style

You might be attracted to one of the defined styles or period styles that are popular in home design. Some are more fashionable than others, and it would be impossible to mention them all in detail. Other styles, like 50s, Art Nouveau, and Art Deco, are very specialized. They are usually picked by people who have a good idea of what was produced in those periods and know exactly what they want a room to look like.

Eclectic styles—those that borrow bits and pieces from all periods—are the hardest to achieve successfully. If you've

confidence, you can mix and match in this way very successfully, and make a 'showpiece' of your home. But this is not what most people want, and the four styles mentioned here should cover the needs of inexperienced home designers who are simply looking for a stylish solution.

If you'd like to find out more about a particular period or style, borrow as many books as you can on the subject, and then imitate. It might be a good idea to consider buying some of these—far from being purely luxury items, they'll always be good reference and interesting reading, and they can be used afterwards as accessories in your living-room scheme. Look in your local library too.

Magazines often show room sets which may provide inspiration. Certain styles are regularly featured in these, and quite often the magazines base their sets around a 'theme' such as a period style. They'll also give you a good idea of the type of shop you might look in.

Invest too in a good book on antiques; if you study it carefully, you'll be able to recognize not only the genuine article, but also good reproductions, which will help if you want your room to look authentic.

You may, of course, want to change styles from room to room, although it is better to have a fairly uniform arrangement in a small house. Owners of larger homes can experiment or change styles more easily, and obviously have more space to adapt rooms to fit the chosen styles.

The modern look

When some people hear the word 'modern' they instantly shy away; and if the phrase 'hi-tech' creeps in, the reaction is even worse! But 'modern' does not have to mean lack of comfort,

Left: Light colours, delicate fabrics and flowers form the basis of the pretty, feminine look of this bedroom. Above: Contrasting textures and natural colours combine with streamlined furniture for a modern look.

even though modern styles are generally plain, simple and uncluttered, with clean, angular lines and functional design.

It is the most practical style that can be used in small homes, but in large rooms too it can look stunning.

Modern style is one of the most labour-saving of all. Most items should be easy to clean, because of the lack of intricate detail on furniture and also the types of materials they are made from.

Colours

Neutral colours form the basis for this style. Often, however, a stronger colour is used to contrast—such as bright red. Certain rooms, like children's bedrooms, can use a combination of bright colours,

and practical, modern furniture is ideal. These rooms tend to be rather timeless since the object is to base them around the children's needs and not necessarily a design medium.

Walls and floors

In the modern look walls tend to be pale and neutral. It is quite acceptable to add texture—by, for example, featuring one wall with its plaster stripped to bare bricks. White, grey and cream are ideal tones, but you can introduce colour into the scheme by using a painting technique like rag-rolling. Such techniques actually go back as far as Victorian times but make wonderful foils for the starkness that modern schemes project. They'll give just a hint of colour to walls in any

style scheme and may help you to compromise if you don't want the total boldness of modern looks.

As space and light are important elements in modern-look homes, open-plan living could be introduced by removing walls, or part of them. You might incorporate dining and living rooms, or even a combination of these plus kitchen for a really airy, spacious feel. However, you should check on building regulations before proceeding on this sort of work.

Floor coverings should be in pale tones, but there's no reason why a colourful, geometric-patterned rug should not be introduced to break up a large expanse of plain floor. If you want to pick an all-over patterned carpet, choose

Left: A neutral colour scheme, plus bare floorboards, exposed brickwork and modern prints in bright accent colours contribute to the cheerful modern décor of this room. Above: This hi-tech living/dining room utilizes glass and chrome with a simple and striking black and off-white colour scheme.

Above: Modern-style rooms can look comfortable and welcoming despite the pale colours if interesting textures are used. Far right: Chrome and glass, and upbeat black and white with tiny flashes of red, make this bedroom a perfect example of modern hi-tech décor.

one that has a fairly subtle, geometric design. Texture can be introduced with plain or shag-pile carpet.

Bare floorboards look very stylish in modern settings. They'll look fine simply sanded and sealed, but you can also stain or varnish them to match the room scheme.

Hallways need really hard-wearing flooring, so sheet vinyl or vinyl tiles in plain colours would be ideal.

Furniture

Modern schemes should have no unnecessary furniture as this would only clutter them up. Each piece should be chosen carefully to fulfil a particular need, and never bought on a whim.

Geometrics, straight lines and angles are more in keeping with this style than a selection of curves and patterns. However, you can relieve what might seem a coldly angular room with a shapely vase or rounded seat cushions.

Natural and man-made materials mix quite happily in furniture and furnishings. Furniture can be made of steel, chrome, aluminium or other metals, glass or moulded plastic like perspex. Natural materials include wool, cotton, cork, stone and all kinds of wood which show their natural grain. A little luxury can be added with pieces in leather, but these tend to be expensive.

Furniture should be low and streamlined. Seldom is a three-piece suite used in modern schemes these days. You're more likely to see compact units grouped in L or U shapes, according to the room. Furniture often takes on a practical, dual role, like the type of seating that doubles as a bed with integrated storage space.

Storage units will have adjustable shelves, drawers and cupboards for flexibility. Small low designs with angular lines make ideal sofa tables and lamp tables. Texture can be introduced using coverings for chairs and sofas of tweedy fabrics, wool, corduroy, linen union, or others.

Storage should be as unobtrusive as possible. It's more in keeping to have one large unit along a wall, rather than lots of small items. Other pieces of furniture that do not fit in the modern style can be painted in pale colours that will help them merge in with the background.

Bedroom furniture may be finished in paler coloured woods like pine, ash,

beech or teak. White melamine can be used to great effect—some ranges are very stylish, and melamine is an extremely practical surface to keep clean.

Windows

An important element of the light, airy, spacious feel of modern-style rooms is the type of window dressings you use. These should be simple and unfussy, and designed to let in as much light as possible during the day.

Roller, Venetian or vertical blinds are ideal because of their clean lines, but there's no reason why curtains should not be hung as well. Pick fabrics in designs to match the geometric lines of the rest of the room, in predominantly plain or neutral colours. Use a tailored heading such as pinch pleats rather than a frilled one.

Accessories

Appropriate light fittings are easy to find. Coolie metal shades in various sizes and colours are perfect for central pendant fittings. For localized lighting, table lamps with square or rectangular bases, spotlights, downlighters and super-luxury standard lamps in futuristic designs will all look stylish and clean.

Pictures will give interest to otherwise rather bare walls. Narrow frames in pale and stark colours or metals like chrome will be most suitable, and it's better to have one large print on the wall than several little ones.

Other accessories might consist of one or two impressive pieces of china, which would be more in keeping than several collections of ornaments scattered about the rooms.

Greenery fits in well with all settings and may add drama and life to a modern scheme. Large potted plants such as Swiss cheese plants and rubber plants are particularly good.

The Victorian look

This is the complete opposite in style to the modern look since, rather than keeping things to a minimum, Victorian themes involve pattern, texture and ornamentation. The Victorians themselves tended to cram their homes with opulence and clutter, which might not appeal so much these days because of the extra work involved in keeping everything clean. In Victorian times it was the servants who had to take care of such possessions!

Nevertheless, it is possible to copy the Victorian look to a large extent, and very successfully, creating the rich and luxurious atmosphere that was enjoyed in the last century.

Architectural details

This rather emphatic design style is best suited to large rooms with high ceilings —invariably only found in older houses. You could fit cornices, ceiling roses, picture rails and dado rails to give the right basic architectural structure around which to work, if you haven't got them already. There are many specialists who make plaster mouldings in traditional styles, or you can achieve similar effects using borders and friezes (see page 37).

Panelled doors were very much part of the Victorian style. If yours have already been replaced by modern doors, you could consider buying traditional panelled doors to fit instead. They are available in a variety of styles. A cheaper alternative would be to keep the flush doors and add detail with strips of beading.

Walls and ceilings

The Victorians were very fond of dark colours, soft, thick textures and a 'twilight' atmosphere in their rooms. This might be a little extreme these days if copied exactly, so you'll need to adapt and modify. Ceilings painted in a light colour will offset such darkness.

There are many modern designs that have been inspired by original Victorian patterns. William Morris was a particular favourite at the time, and genuine copies of his designs and Morris-type patterns can be found. There are also light variations on traditional Victorian designs which give the atmosphere without looking too heavy.

Small bedrooms or living rooms decorated with a small-scale patterned floral paper plus appropriate accessories will create the correct effect.

The Victorians tended to use colour and pattern combinations that clashed—probably because the lighting in those days was so bad. Now there is not only more choice, but you can choose permutations of designs to create the right atmosphere without actually offending your colour sense.

Windows

Lace, velvet and brocade curtains are the most authentic fabrics for use on windows. The real thing tends to be expensive, but there are lots of synthetic versions available which can look equally

Below: Dark walls, lace curtains and a beautiful crochet bedspread re-create the style of soft furnishing that the Victorians favoured in their bedrooms.

good. If you don't want full, heavy curtains, fake side ones will create the right style and take up considerably less fabric. But if you're worried about heat retention, full curtains will be best.

Brass was much in evidence and can be used for curtain poles. Alternatively, use dark, wooden versions such as walnut or mahogany finish. The ornately carved wooden pelmets of Victorian times would be difficult to achieve now, but a less elaborate design could be used instead.

Accessories
Reproduction light fittings of the right style are easily available, whether you want chandeliers, brass wall lights, white round glass ceiling globes or imitation oil-lamp styles. Antique oil lamps also fit in beautifully. Silk, or silk effect shades with fringes should be used on table lamps. Candlesticks in brass and china will not only provide attractive accessories but will be most useful for romantic dinner parties.

Wall mounted mirrors are a must for this style—no Victorian room was without one. Original ones tend to be costly, but reproductions can be found that are less expensive. Old gilt mirrors in poor condition can be resilvered, and you can restore the frames quite easily with a little bit of elbow grease and a tin of gold artists' paint. So look around secondhand and antique shops and auction rooms for bargains.

If you don't have a fireplace but want to add one, mantelpieces and accessories can be bought in the correct style from specialist shops. Otherwise, restore those you have to look as traditionally Victorian as possible. You don't have to light the fire—simply use it as a decorative surround. Alternatively, real flame-effect gas fires look most authentic and usually come with a choice of quite stunning ornamental grates, fire irons

(very important), fire dogs, fenders and so on. Always use a fireguard if you have children.

Rich use of fabrics and tassels will make a bedroom authentic-looking. Use lace, if you can afford it, to cover beds, dress the windows or drape over furniture.

Furniture
Victorian furniture tended to be big—too much so for modern living, as it would waste valuable living room space. However, modern sofas come in many

styles and, covered in an appropriate fabric, would suffice.

Other pieces of furniture you could consider are wing chairs, sideboards, and upright chairs in rosewood or mahogany (or lighter woods stained to create the right tones).

Small corner tables are typically Victorian and were much used to display family photographs, china and other ornaments.

No living room was complete without its aspidistra—you might invest in one for a very authentic, charming touch.

Left: The central feature of this Victorian-style bedroom is the brass bed, which demands slightly ornate traditional furniture as well as embellished mirrors and pictures with heavy frames placed quite high on the walls. To show up these accessories colours are subdued. Above: A purple satin seat-cover on a wickerwork chair, set off by mixed patterns, makes an interesting Victorian-style feature.

Above: This small cane table is just right for an Oriental-style room, and it is easily made from bamboo cane, plywood and woven cane mesh.

The Oriental look

Simplicity is the key to achieving the Oriental look. Rather than the strong, simplistic lines that make up the modern style, however, the emphasis is on tranquillity and harmony in Oriental-type rooms. Rooms are very much in keeping with Oriental philosophy—that furniture, accessories and schemes should be at peace with their surroundings. This means using soft pastel or natural shades, with surfaces uncluttered and almost stark.

Oriental-type furniture and furnishings are very widely available and within the reach of most people's pockets. Obviously some pieces like authentic Chinese rugs and certain Oriental lacquerwork are still costly. But these are real investments and may be considered when you want to really splash out, later.

Walls, windows and floors

Subtle wallpapers are ideal—for example, designs which introduce pale, random colour on a plain background. Walls painted white are in keeping with this style as well, and indeed provide the ideal uncomplicated background for accessories.

Silk is an extremely appropriate, natural fabric to use in an Oriental-style room—but it is very expensive. You could compromise by using small amounts of it for cushions. If you can afford it, wallhangings made of silk would look lovely.

Pinoleum, bamboo or split-cane blinds are just right for windows. Alternatively, make Roman blinds from plain fabrics or those that use simple designs. Leave them unlined and they'll have a translucent quality.

Ideally, floors should be covered with matting of some kind, such as rush, coir or sisal, but you may think these a little uncomfortable, especially if you've young children. You can use carpet, as long as you pick one in a natural colour like cream or pale beige, but make sure it has an unobtrusive pile.

Furniture

Furniture should not be a problem—bamboo, cane, and real and fake lacquerwork are all easily found. If you don't know where to begin, local department stores might be visited, as they usually stock quite a wide range of such pieces.

Real lacquerwork furniture is a luxury, as it can be very expensive, but some imitations are quite acceptable, and you can imitate it fairly successfully by painting small items of wood furniture with black, crimson or cinnamon gloss paint. Put on several thin coats for a really hard shine—real lacquerwork uses layers and layers of varnish, dried in special conditions to give the high gloss effect.

Bamboo is another material that lots of furniture is made from in the Oriental style. It's usually quite cheap and you can add big, squashy cushions to add comfort if it seems a little hard.

Bedroom and dining furniture, bookshelves and display units are easily found in appropriate materials. Rattan tables are ideal; these are often stocked in furniture stores or small local shops, with chairs to match.

Screens are perfect for this style of decoration. Best suited for a living room are those using wood or lacquerwork. You can make your own from wood. Paint it black gloss and attach Oriental style patterned fabric to the panels with tacks, upholstery studs or a staple gun. Bamboo and cane screens are also ideal.

Futons are probably the most authentic style of bed. They are simple in design, with the mattress laid on a floor-standing wooden frame. They can be very comfortable (see page 89).

Accessories

Accessories are easy to find and very varied. Paper lampshades, paper wall hangings, fans, kites, carved soapstone, jade, and some porcelain and bone china are all suitable.

Many large china departments have special Oriental displays, stocking, among hundreds of other appropriate items, Japanese tea sets consisting of a teapot (usually with cane or bamboo handle) and cups. Many also come with matching rice bowls and spoons. Any of these make ideal accessories for the Oriental look and are practical too, since Chinese food and tea are ever-popular, and there's nothing like eating and drinking it from the real thing.

Left and above: Lacquerwork and other high-gloss finishes are important elements of the Oriental look, yet they blend equally well with conventional Western furnishings.

Right: Rough walls, rustic shelving and natural colours are the right background for collections of nick-nacks in a country-style home, and organized clutter is a feature of this type of décor.

The country look

Comfort and natural living are the basic elements in the country look; there are no hard and fast rules, since the style evolves from various sources rather than one defined set of designs.

The country look is not expensive to achieve, nor restricting. This alone puts some people off, since it is not considered particularly 'stylish' in the traditional sense.

Because it is based around such a mixture of colours, designs, textures and patterns, the country look can appear to some degree cluttered and unruly. Because of this, rooms need extra attention to stay looking good; this means regular tidying and dusting.

Small, low-ceilinged rooms are absolutely ideal for the country style. They are usually without the elaborate architectural details like cornices and mouldings that ruin the natural effect. If your ceiling is too high and you really want to go the whole way in achieving a country look, consider installing a false, lower one. You can even add imitation beams for the finishing touch.

Walls and fabrics

Walls should be unsophisticated—either painted white or pale cream. Matt emulsion gives the right 'rough' look, while bare brickwork and rough plaster are both well suited to the image. Some wallcoverings are ideal, like woodchip or hessian painted a pale tone so that the texture is brought to life.

Clear pastel colours are also fine. If you're not sure which colours to use, follow nature for inspiration. In other areas, fibres such as cotton, wood, slate, stone, rush and cane are natural agents for this style; at all costs avoid glass and steel.

If you like handicrafts, you could make

woods will seem out of place. Teak will definitely look far too modern, as will metals and shining finishes.

To set the right mood add some traditional pieces such as rocking chairs, dressers and chests in suitable woods. Brass is fine, and a bedroom will be given the correct style if you add a brass bedstead, or one made from wood. Unfortunately, these tend to be expensive, so you could pick a conventional bed, disguise it with bedspread and valance, and make your own headboard from quilting attached to a brass pole.

Left and above: The stripped pine refectory table is a must for any country-style home, and simple ladderback chairs, old pine dressers and settles, plus baskets and dried flowers or herbs all contribute to the effect.

your own patchwork items such as bedspreads, sofa covers, rugs. Gingham is another natural and can be used for tablelinen, curtains or cushions.

If you really prefer to paper your walls, then at least go easy on the pattern. The less formal the design the better, so tiny florals are ideal especially in bedrooms.

Furniture

Furniture should be simple and practical, yet solid and sturdy. Woods such as pine, beech, elm and birch can be used, or a few of the darker ones like oak may be incorporated. You can stain very pale woods a darker colour to fit in, but richer and more formal mahoganies and rose-

Living in style

Right: Exposed timbers, bare brickwork, sanded-and-sealed floorboards and textured natural fabrics give an authentic country-style feel to this converted boat-house, and the modern accessories blend in perfectly well.

Chairs and sofas must be comfortable, for this is the essence of country living. If the upholstery is out of keeping, you could re-cover them with loose covers in a floral pattern and add masses of squashy cushions.

Unlike other looks, heights and styles do not need to match exactly, so choosing furniture is much easier.

Floors and windows

Floors look best in natural materials like stone, brick or quarry tiles. Add softness with matting or rugs, strewn about the floor. If you have wooden floors, sand and seal them and add a mellow-toned varnish. Of course carpet can be used, but pick one with a short twist pile. Wool carpets are best, but you can use mixes as long as they look woolly.

Windows should be fitted with a pretty treatment. Lace is ideal, with curtains tied back during the day. Austrian blinds will look soft and full. Always pick traditional headings, with poles and tracks in brass and wood—never plastic.

Curtains can be made of any natural fabric, such as cotton or chintz, and soft floral patterns are fine.

Accessories

Traditional light fittings look good. Some of the designs that are suitable for Victorian-style rooms are equally appropriate here, such as brass oil lamps, hanging capiz shell shades and pottery-base table lamps.

Look around secondhand shops for functional objects that can be displayed as accessories, like milk urns, stools, tapestry frames and kitchen utensils and implements. Framed portraits and country scene paintings are perfect.

An open fire is obviously a vital element for this style and should be made into a focal point. However, if you don't have one, a wood-burning stove will

provide an equally attractive alternative. You can add appropriate homely accessories like a log basket or a brass coal bucket and the inevitable fire-irons.

Plants, fresh and dried flowers, corn dollies, baskets, are all in keeping. You could try pressing and drying your own flowers for decoration and getting into homely crafts such as jam-making and bread-baking to add to the atmosphere of comfort and welcome.

Above: A hand-painted wooden bedstead is a lovely addition to any country-style bedroom, and the matching bedside chest and old-fashioned sampler echo the same theme.

Index

A

Accessories 96–105, 110, 113, 115, 119
Alcoves 27, 66
Austrian blinds 51

B

Basement conversions 70, 71
Beams, exposed 42, 118
Bedrooms 85–95, 101–5, 110
  children's 89, 91, 94–5, 103–5
  lighting for 28–30
  multi-purpose 72–3
Beds 85–90, 95, 117
  fold-away 65
  on a platform 62, 64
  sofa 64–5
Bedside lighting 28
Bed-sitters, improving 63
Blinds 44, 49–51, 110, 114
Bookshelves 18, 63
Borders 36, 54, 58
Brickwork, exposed 36, 42, 105, 109, 118

C

Carpets 33–5, 59
Carpet tiles 34
Ceilings 41–2
  false 23, 24, 42
  illuminated 24
  lowering or raising visually 17, 25, 42
  tented 42
Cellars
  conversion of 70, 71
  lighting for 28
Chairs 76–80
Cladding
  brick 36
  stone 36
  tongue-and-groove 41, 42
Cloakroom, downstairs, adding 56, 71, 73
Collections, displaying 98–9
Colour 6–11
Colour boards 11
Colour schemes 7, 8, 9, 10–11, 109
  effects of 17, 24, 58
  lighting for 24
  for size of room 17, 18
Cork door covering 54

Cork wallcovering 41
Cornices 37, 42
Country-style furnishings 116–19
Coziness, creating 18, 24, 39, 79
Curtains 17, 44–9, 53, 66, 112–13, 119
Cushions, floor 62, 78

D

Dados and dado rails 37, 39, 40, 57, 58
Design and planning 14, 75; *see also* Colour schemes *and* Styles, furnishing
Dhurries 36, 79
Dimmer switches 24, 30
Dining rooms
  furnishing 37, 80–2, 84–5, 105
  lighting for 22, 27–8
Displays
  of collections 98–9
  of pictures 99–101, 105
Doors 53–4, 112
  blocking up 16, 17
  rehanging 17, 54
  replacing 17, 53–4, 112
  use of glass with 18, 20, 54, 56
Downlighters 22, 23, 24, 27
Dressers 75, 85, 117

E

Extensions 66, 70

F

Fabrics
  for ceiling covering 42
  co-ordinating with wallpaper 12
  for curtains 17, 44
  for lampshades 27
  for sofas and armchairs 17, 76
  types of 79
  for wallcoverings 41, 62
Felt wallcoverings 41
Festoon blinds 51
Fireplaces 14, 17, 97, 113, 119
Flats, rented, improving 61–3
Floors and floor coverings 32–6, 59, 109–10, 114, 119
Focal points 14, 16, 17, 49
Furniture 74–95, 110, 113, 114, 117–19
  arranging 14, 17, 18

fabrics for 17, 76
suitability of 17

G

Glass 20
  furniture 18, 20, 81, 82, 109, 110
  painted 20
  stained 20
  use of with doors 18, 20, 54, 56

H

Halls 27, 55–9
Headboards 89–90
Hessian wallcoverings 41, 58
Hi-tech décor 107, 109, 110
Houseplants 97, 105, 109

L

Lacquerwork, real or imitation 114
Lamps and lampshades 22, 25, 27, 102, 105
Landings 55–9
Lighting and light fittings 21–30, 56–7, 109, 119
  antique or reproduction 25, 30, 113
  ceiling 23, 24, 25, 27
  childproof 28–30
  concealed 25
  fluorescent 22, 24, 28
  tungsten 28
Living rooms 75–81, 82–4, 105
  lighting for 22, 27, 28
Loft conversions 66, 68, 69
Louvred doors 54, 92
Louvred shutters 51–2, 53

M

Mirror 18–19, 41, 54, 57, 113
Modern-style furnishings 107–11
Mouldings, plaster 37, 42
Murals, hand-painted 37–9

N

Noticeboards 59, 99

O

Oil lamps 25, 30, 113
One-room living 63–6
Open-plan living 18, 56, 62, 66, 84, 109
Oriental-style furnishings 114–15

P

Paints 36
Panelling 41, 42
Panels, wall 37
Partitions 61, 64
Patterns
  in carpets 34
  effects of 12, 18, 34
  mixing 11, 12, 40
  in upholstery fabrics 79
Pelmets 47
  with concealed lighting 25
Picture rails 18, 37
Pictures, displaying 58, 62, 99–101, 105
Pinboards and noticeboards 59, 99
Piping, use of 47, 76
Platform, building bed on 62, 63

R

Radiators 47, 105
Rented accommodation 61–3
Roller blinds 49–50
Roman blinds 50–1
Room dividers 61, 62, 64, 73, 84
Rooms
  altering size or shape of visually 17, 18, 20, 25, 34, 42
  aspect, effect of 10
  changing functions of 14, 61
  knocking through 17, 61, 109
  multi-level 62, 63
  planning and furnishing 14–18, 75–95, 106–19
  sub-dividing 61, 64
  see also Bedrooms, Dining rooms, Halls *and* Living rooms
Rugs 35–6, 103

S

Screens 53, 62, 64, 73, 114
Seating 76–80
Shelving systems 84–5, 95, 98
Shutters 51–3
Sofas 76–9
Space
  increasing illusion of 17, 20, 34
  utilizing 56, 59, 61, 72, 73
Spotlights 22, 25, 27, 28, 30
Staircases 55–9
  utilizing space under 71–2, 73
Stencilling 32, 36, 42, 80

Storage 56, 57, 61, 66, 83–5, 90–4, 110
Styles, furnishing 75, 106–19

T

Tables 80–3
Tie-backs, curtain 47
Tiles
  carpet 34
  ceramic 33
  mirror 18–19, 41, 57
Trompe l'oeil 37–9

U

Uplighters 22, 25, 27

V

Valances 44, 47
Venetian blinds 51
Victorian-style furnishings 112–13
Vinyl floor coverings 32–3
Vinyl wallpapers 39

W

Wallcoverings 36–41, 57–9, 62, 109, 112, 114, 116–17
Wall lights 22
Wallpaper 11, 39–41, 112, 114
  borders 36, 54, 58
  co-ordinating with fabric 12
  effects of different designs 12, 18
Walls
  removing 17, 18, 56, 61, 109
  sloping 66, 68, 69, 70
  uneven 36
Wardrobes 20, 61, 66, 90–2, 93
Waterbeds 89
Windows 16, 44–53, 66, 109, 110, 112–113, 114, 119
  arched 53
  bay 49, 53, 61
  casement 53
  circular 44, 53
  French 53
  internal 20
  picture 53
  roof 51, 66
  sash 53
  small, enlarging visually 17–18, 44
  tall and thin, widening visually 44
Wood floors 32
Wood panelling 41, 42